ADVANCE PRAISE FOR *THE GAME PLAN*

"You may beat your demon the first time through *The Game Plan* or you may need it through a long season, but it's a worthy companion. Joe's advice is sound and his format is friendly."

> — Tom Minnery
> Focus on the Family

"Joe Dallas has written a practical handbook for men who want to get serious about their purity. *The Game Plan* is the tool that answers one of the most troubling problems in the church today, and it does so with compassion, clarity, and a sound biblical base."

> — D. James Kennedy. Ph.D.
> Senior Minister
> Coral Ridge Presbyterian Church

"For more than a decade Joe Dallas has been a role model for those battling to overcome sexual addiction as well as to those ministering to the sexually broken. *The Game Plan* is one more example of how God is using him to bring freedom to the captives. I know Joe. I trust Joe. What he says lines up with God's word and when put to practice, bears much fruit."

> — Alan Chambers
> President
> Exodus International

"Joe Dallas gives readers a much needed plan for battling pornography and sexual addiction. *The Game Plan* will give you the tools necessary to stop looking at pornography and never return. A must read!"

> — Craig Gross
> Founder of XXXchurch.com
> Author of *Questions You Can't Ask Your Mama* and *The Gutter*

THE GAME PLAN

JOE DALLAS

THOMAS NELSON
Since 1798

NASHVILLE DALLAS MEXICO CITY RIO DE JANEIRO

Published in Nashville, Tennessee, by Thomas Nelson. Thomas Nelson is a registered trademark of Thomas Nelson, Inc.

Thomas Nelson, Inc., titles may be purchased in bulk for educational, business, fund-raising, or sales promotional use. For information, please e-mail SpecialMarkets@ThomasNelson.com.

All Scripture quotations, unless otherwise indicated, are taken from The New King James Version®, © 1979, 1980, 1982, Thomas Nelson, Inc., Publishers. Used by permission. All rights reserved. Scriptures marked KJV are taken from the King James Version of the Bible. Scriptures marked NIV are taken from The Holy Bible, New International Version®. © 1973, 1978, 1984 by International Bible Society. Used by permission of Zondervan. All rights reserved.

ROUTE— Repentance, Order, Understanding, Training, Endurance—is a trademark of Joe Dallas. All rights reserved.

ISBN 978-0-8499-0633-6 (TP)

Library of Congress Cataloging-in-Publication Data

Dallas, Joe, 1954–
    The game plan / Joe Dallas.
      p. cm.
    includes bibliographical references.
    ISBN 978-0-8499-0633-6
    1. Christian men—Religious life. 2. Sex—Religious aspects—Christianity. 3. Chasity.
I. Title.
BV4528.2.D35 2005
241'.66—dc22   2005010011

Printed in the United States of America

10 11 12 WC 15 14 13

For my beloved son Jeremy—

May you always be a Player, conqueror, and lover of God.

CONTENTS

Introduction   ix

Before We Begin   xxiii

Qualities of a Player   xxv

REPENTANCE

Day 1   Recruitment: Getting Back into the Game   3

Day 2   Action Plan for Recruitment   12

Day 3   Crisis: Truth Hurts   15

Day 4   Action Plan for Crisis   23

Day 5   Separation: Making the Final Cut   26

Day 6   Action Plan for Separation   32

ORDER

Day 7   Structure: Your Daily Meds   43

Day 8   Action Plan for Structure   57

Day 9   Alignment: Teammates and Allies   59

Day 10   Action Plan for Alignment   68

Day 11   Confession and Restitution   72

Day 12   Action Plan for Confession and Restitution 82

UNDERSTANDING

Day 13 The Arena and the Opposition   89

Day 14 Action Plan for the Arena   103

Day 15 The Wounded Player   105

Day 16 Action Plan for Healing   115

Day 17 Understanding Temptation   119

Day 18 Action Plan for Understanding Temptation   128

TRAINING

Day 19 Temptation-Resistance Techniques   133

Day 20 Action Plan for Resisting Temptation   147

Day 21 Entitlement   150

Day 22 Action Plan for Overcoming Entitlement   161

Day 23 Boundaries   163

Day 24 Action Plan for Developing Boundaries   174

ENDURANCE

Day 25 In Case of Relapse   179

Day 26 Action Plan for Relapse Contingency   190

Day 27 Your Broader Purpose   192

Day 28 Action Plan for Your Broader Purpose   200

Day 29 Conversion and Epiphany   202

Day 30 Action Plan for Epiphany   211

        Appendix: Questions Players Frequently Ask   213

        Notes   223

INTRODUCTION

A famous Christian long ago told us that when he was a young man he prayed constantly for chastity; but years later he realized that while his lips had been saying, "Oh Lord, make me chaste," his heart had been secretly adding, "But please don't do it just yet."

—C. S. Lewis, *Mere Christianity*

Since you picked up this book, my guess is you're either in crisis over your sexual behavior, or you want to avoid ever having that sort of crisis.

And why shouldn't you? You've got other plans, after all—a family, a home, or a career. Or maybe you plan to earn a degree or complete some other project or achievement. At the very least, I figure you want someone to love, decent health, and enough money to pay the bills. And by now you've probably attained some of those goals, so I'll also assume you've steered your life in a certain direction, and to some extent, you've succeeded.

You have expectations, too, especially of yourself. You expect to be a certain type of man—not perfect, but the kind of man you can respect. You want to be a guy who lives up to his beliefs, has a decent reputation, and is the sort of friend, father, and husband who makes his loved ones feel safe and cared for. And if you do ever wind up having any deep, dark secrets, you figure they'll be the sort that aren't really *that* deep and dark.

Plans and expectations—since you've got both, the last thing you want is to see them derailed by a moral failure. So maybe you picked up *The Game Plan* to make sure that never happens.

Then again, maybe it already has happened. Maybe it started so long ago it's hard to recall how or when, but at some point you discovered "it." We usually refer to "it" as sexual sin or acting out. However you label "it," it's the thing that's now disrupting your life so badly you're willing to pick up this book.

The form "it" takes varies from man to man. For many, it's a combination of pornography and sexual fantasies. Others find it in a prostitute's embrace, strip clubs, adulterous or premarital sex, anonymous encounters, phone sex, cybersex, or chat rooms. Maybe you've practiced it in less common ways, through some habit or private ritual you're deeply ashamed of and have never admitted to anyone. (Although heaven knows, there really is nothing new under the sun, and I can guarantee you've neither discovered nor created a new sin.)

But whatever its form, it has become part of your life, despite your plans and expectations, because in its own strange way, it *works.*

When you discovered it, you found something that delivered both meaning and ecstasy. *Meaning* isn't normally a word we associate with immorality, but think about it: there really can be profound meaning in actions that are completely wrong. Just because they're meaningful doesn't make them right. But just because they're wrong doesn't remove the sense of meaning. In plain language, if sexual sin wasn't deeply meaningful in some way, men wouldn't indulge it.

Masturbating to Internet pornography, for example, can bring a man comfort, thrill, power, and escape, all of which create a meaningful (though unhealthy) experience. When you add ecstasy to the mix—the anticipation of seeing the porn, the adrenaline rush that comes with viewing erotic images, the heightened sensations building up to orgasm, then the orgasm itself—then you've got yourself a powerful product. Morally wrong? Sure. Addictive, even destructive? Absolutely. But powerful, nonetheless. And when a customer tries a product that delivers both meaning and ecstasy, there's a good chance he'll go back for seconds.

But it didn't stop at "seconds," did it? Maybe it became a fairly regular part of your routine. Oh, there may have been times—months, even years—when you stopped. But then it kept returning;

or, I should say, you kept returning to it. It was reliable and ever-present, like an old friend who never said no. So it became not only a secret vice, but a secret *de*vice as well—a product you've relied on for comfort, connection, and escape.

But knowing your behavior was wrong hasn't stopped you from repeating it. And repeating it did not, at least in the beginning, ruin your plans and expectations. While nursing your sin, you may have also built up that family, career, and life you were aiming for. The sin didn't keep it from happening. There's a good chance, in fact, you've told yourself, "This is wrong, but it isn't *that* wrong! If I'm careful and discreet, it won't interfere with the rest of my life. I am, after all, a good man in general; and even good men can have a few bad habits."

Then something happened. You got caught, perhaps, or at least had a close call. Maybe your situation is worse—an arrest, a sexually transmitted disease, professional or financial damage—and now your life has been thrown into endless somersaults. Or maybe you're just exhausted from the lying, double-mindedness, and shame that come from prolonged sexual sin. Whatever the case, a crisis of truth has gotten your attention, slapping you in the face with a realization: "This has to stop. I have to change."

Your Life Is Being Interrupted

I say all of this because I know we don't usually ask for help (which is what you're doing by picking up this book) unless a fire has been lit under us. So I doubt that I'm assuming too much in saying you're a man in crisis, either because of what you've done or what you fear doing.

And since you can see by this book's cover that it's written from a biblical perspective, I feel safe in also assuming you're a Christian. In that case, your crisis springs not just from circumstance but from deep within as well.

Because you know better. You know God, you know something about His will for your life, and you know His will can't include behavior the Bible so strongly and specifically condemns. In light of that, you know what you need to *avoid* doing. Or, if you're already doing it, you know what you need to *stop* doing.

You need to stop using pornography. You need to break off the adulterous, casual, or premarital sexual relationship. You need to distance yourself from the actions that have created your crisis, actions that may have been meaningful but have also done more damage than you ever thought they would. You need to stop, and you need to stop now.

But even knowing that may not have stopped you so far. Maybe (in fact, probably) you don't need to know *what* to stop doing. You need to know *how* to stop doing it.

I've yet to meet a Christian in sexual sin who didn't know what he should or shouldn't do. Most of us, after all, have spent years hearing that sexual contact before or apart from marriage is wrong. So it's not the knowledge of right from wrong you're look-ing for, but a plan—a game plan that will map out a practical, effective way to recover (and keep) your sexual integrity.

Now you have one. *The Game Plan* is written for the Christian man who is tempted by sexual sin or who has gotten involved in it but is now ready to walk away from it, and who wants a practical, biblically based plan to guide him.

Since 1987, I've had the honor of working with these men through private counseling and retreat seminars. I've admired their courage in admitting they had a problem, and I've learned from them, as together we've found answers and tools. I've also noticed similarities in their lives and circumstances, four of which you might relate to.

First, their introduction to sexual sin came early in life. Lost innocence has been a common theme: childhood exposure to pornography, preadolescent sexual experiments, or even molesta-tion. They saw too much too soon, and they explored too early. Masturbation, pornography, and sexual fantasies were incorporated into their lifestyle, and while many never had sex with another per-son until their adulthood, many others, in fact, were promiscuous while still teenagers. They found "it" while they were young; they indulged it frequently.

Second, despite their sexual behavior, these men had a genuine and abiding faith in Christ. Whether raised in the church or converted later, these were not men who just pretended to be Christians. They were true believers: born again, belonging to a local congregation, and, in many ways, committed to their faith. I haven't needed to share the gospel with them, since they already knew and responded to it long before we met. Most were active in their churches; many were elders, music ministers, deacons, or board members. More than a few have been pastors.

Which leads to a third common characteristic: their conversion experience, though genuine, did not make their sexual problems disappear. All too often they thought it would, so they expected God to provide a sort of microwave experience, rapidly cooking the lust and sinful tendencies right out of them.

But it didn't happen that way. So when those tendencies returned (if indeed they ever left), they decided they must be doing something wrong. "If I'm still tempted to commit the sexual sins I committed before," they reasoned, "then I lack faith, or I'm not trying hard enough, or there's something radically flawed about me as a man."

They're wrong, of course, but the silence in the church about sexual sin only confirms their fears. How often, really, do we hear Christians talk openly about the problem of sexual temptation? When did you last hear, even in the privacy of small prayer and Bible study groups, someone say, "I'm wrestling with sexual temptations; please pray for me"? And when sexual sin becomes a sermon topic, isn't it more often than not referred to as a problem outside the church, rather than a common weakness we ourselves need to guard against?

All of this can leave a man thinking he's the only Christian with sexual temptations, which doubles his shame. The shame encourages his isolation and secrecy—twin elements that make a man's heart a lonely, dark, and fertile place where sexual sin can take root, grow, and thrive.

It's thrived in so many of the men I've worked with, sometimes for years, until the fourth characteristic finally came into play: exposure leading to motivation.

Virtually every man I've worked with has had a crisis, whether in his conscience or his circumstances, that forced the problem into the light. And with that exposure came fear, anger, or deep dissatisfaction. These, in turn, became strong incentives for change. By the time I've met these men, they usually are highly motivated, humbled by their sin, teachable, and ready to work.

If these characteristics come close to describing you, and if you, too, are motivated and ready to work, then I look forward to spending the next thirty days walking with you into a healthier, godly lifestyle.

I Remember, and I Regret

In case you're wondering, yes, I've been there, done that. Sexual sin has played a major, devastating role in my life, so for me this isn't academic. It's deeply personal, and oddly enough, even after years of talking about it publicly, I still wince and feel an ache in my gut as I write about it.

Sexual desire and spiritual hunger have been two of the most powerful forces shaping my life. They've often been at war, and at times I've tried to kill one in the interest of satisfying the other. Neither died, and only later in life did I realize neither was meant to. One, instead, was meant to live in subjection to the other, a subjection that wouldn't come until I was nearly thirty years old.

The war started early, and badly. I was exposed to porn at age eight by a man who used it as a device to seduce and molest me. He spotted me in the lobby of a theater, befriended me, and gained my trust. Like most pedophiles, he knew a vulnerable kid when he saw one. So up to the moment he pushed me into a bathroom stall and pulled off my shirt, I just thought he was a nice guy who liked me.

The molestations continued for two years and came to include other men as well. By the time they ended, I'd been exposed to sights and experiences that would hugely pervert my view of relationships. Love meant sex, I came to believe. Men were gods, women were objects, and physical beauty was power. These were the dark lessons I gleaned from porn and violation, and they left me a jaded, very broken little boy.

The contrast between those experiences and the way I was raised couldn't have been starker. My parents reared my brothers and me with the morals and discipline that mark a normal home, and the upper-middle-class neighborhood I grew up in was comfortable and attractive. But the best upbringing cannot guarantee safety. I'd ventured naively into something no child should see, though too many see it daily; and when it happened, I assumed it was my own fault. So the habit of keeping my sex life secret and hidden began years before I should even have known what sex was.

I continued using porn, which at that time (the mid-1960s) meant *Playboy* magazine. I learned to steal it from the lower shelves of liquor stores and stuff it under my T-shirt, then bicycle away and spend hours in my homemade fort studying the pictures. The bodies fascinated me, and I loved creating sexual scenes in my mind, scenes in which I was the perfect lover, the ultimate stud—which, after all, I'd learned a man should be. By the time I reached puberty, I was spending hours each week in isolation, poring over my growing collection of erotica.

Sexual experimentation with classmates followed in junior high school, and my first fumbling experience with intercourse came in the ninth grade. By high school I was also having sex with other boys and, occasionally, adult men. If by this point you're getting nauseous, I can only say that even I am a little amazed at how far my downward spiral went.

All of that stopped when, during my junior year, a beautiful classmate invited me to a Bible study. Having no clue what a Bible study was didn't deter me, since there weren't many places I wouldn't have gone with her. But what I found that night forever interrupted my life. I was exposed to the gospel, a message that hounded me for months until I said yes to it. So at sixteen I was born again, and my relationship with Christ took precedence over everything.

Of course, my porn was thrown out and my lifestyle changed as I gave myself over to discipleship. I couldn't get enough Bible study, worship, or prayer, and I became known at my school as a very outspoken "Jesus freak." I deserved the title—I witnessed relentlessly, carrying an enormous Thompson Chain Reference Bible everywhere and viewing every class or lunch break as yet another opportunity to testify. I was sincere, though misguided and, I'm sure, offensive at times in my zeal. But I loved Jesus Christ simply and passionately. Through Him I'd gotten a taste of renewed innocence and purpose, and as the first two years of my Christian life passed, I felt called to translate that love into service. That, ironically, is when the trouble started.

I began volunteering at a newly formed church, playing the piano and teaching Bible studies, when I turned eighteen. This church developed its leaders through an apprenticeship system (seminary was frowned on as legalistic and man-made), and I was soon inducted into full-time ministry. My gifts as a teacher and musician were blossoming, but they bloomed against the backdrop of some frightening inner turmoil because, yet again, I had a secret.

I had by no means returned to porn or fornication of any kind. But I was still lusting, fantasizing, and occasionally masturbating, and I was monstrously disappointed in myself for that. As a minister, I felt I never should have a sexual temptation. No one told me that, and, in fact, it flew in the face of what I read in the Bible about temptation. Still, I expected a full deliverance from lust and all forms of sensual pull. Nothing less was acceptable; anything less made me anxious.

See if you can't relate to this: the more anxious I was about my lust, the more I lusted to ease the anxiety. The more I lusted to alleviate anxiety, the more ashamed I was of myself, which generated (duh!) more anxiety.

It's a cycle known to addicts of all sorts—temptation, indulgence, then shame and anxiety, followed by the temptation to indulge again to kill the shame and anxiety. I could only run on that treadmill for so long before something gave out.

My integrity turned out to be that "something." I was disillusioned by the ministry I'd joined, which had become large and, to my thinking, way too commercial. I planned on finding a secular job and, at the same time, developed a curiosity about the new phenomenon called "adult bookstores." Shortly before leaving the ministry for good, I finally stepped into one, which was akin to a cocaine addict taking his first snort after years of sobriety.

Crossing the threshold of the porn shop was like hitting a wall of dense, tangible lust. Panoramic images of every sexual act imaginable covered the walls, pumping mile-a-minute adrenaline into my brain and flooding me with the old dark magic I'd avoided so long. I stayed for hours, viewing films and browsing magazines, drinking in the toxic rush.

I returned the next night, hired a hooker the night after, and then mapped out every porn shop in the city for a week-long binge. Then, within months, I began an adulterous relationship with the wife of a married friend. She became pregnant, aborted our baby, and ended the affair. I was drinking heavily by then, angry at the world, and sexually insatiable. I began visiting gay bars, I became involved with the owner of one, and rumors soon leaked that Joe Dallas was indescribably backslidden.

During the next six years, I confirmed all of those rumors. Countless partners, anonymous encounters, brief relationships, group sex, and the steady, almost daily diet of pornography made up what I now call my "deathstyle." It was interrupted, thank God, in early 1984, when God sent me a quiet but piercing crisis of truth. I was exhausted, and I began missing so many things I'd thrown away: intimacy with God, good friends, fellowship, and a stable life. And when I compared what I had to the fellowship and peace I'd discarded, I realized I was a victim of my own massive, stupid ripoff.

MAKING OUR WAY BACK

All of this is a lengthy way of saying I've been there. I've probably failed more miserably than you; I know what it's like to say, as did the prodigal son, "I've wasted so much that's good and have so little to show for it." And I understand very well the shame of failure and the hunger for change.

I also know there's a way out, and I want to explore it with you. Follow The Game Plan, and in thirty days things *will* change. That's not because this book offers a quick fix, but because it offers the right steps. I've walked it, taught it, and seen it in action. It's drawn from journals I kept during the three years I spent with a Christian counselor after my repentance and from notes and observations I've made when comparing my own process with the experiences of the men I've worked with as a counselor. I've taught these principles in churches and seminars since 1987; and in 2001, I converted them into a five-day retreat seminar that was attended by more than forty guys each month for three years. More important, though, is the fact that these principles are drawn from, and stick to, biblical principles and practices.

So what exactly *is* The Game Plan? Let's define it by first defining The Game then by naming the phases of The Game and explaining the plan we'll follow while walking through each phase.

DEFINING THE GAME

The Game is the contest you enter into when you commit yourself to purity. When you regularly give in to sexual sin, you in essence go with the flow of the world, the flesh, and even Satan. No contest there—you surrendered. Paul describes this surrender pretty well to the Ephesians when he refers to their past: "You once walked according to the course of this world, according to the prince of the power of the air, the spirit who now works in the sons of disobedience, among whom also we all once conducted ourselves in the lusts of our flesh, fulfilling the desires of the flesh and of the mind, and were by nature children of wrath, just as the others" (2:2–3).

In other words, when you compromise, you cooperate with the enemy. But when you turn away from that cooperation and enter The Game, you initiate a lifelong battle. Your flesh still exists, the world is still a minefield of temptations, and Satan is alive and well and more determined than ever to snare you. So by deciding to change, you've offended all three, and you can expect to be duking them out for as long as you and they exist. So let's accept this hard truth right off the bat: when you pursue godliness by rejecting sexual sin, life gets tough, because now you're fighting the very thing you used to indulge.

I like the way the apostle Paul puts it: "Therefore do not let sin reign in your mortal body, that you should obey it in its lusts. And do not present your members as instruments of unrighteousness to sin, but present yourselves to God as being alive from the dead, and your members as instruments of righteousness to God" (Romans 6:12–13).

By yielding your members in a completely different way, you're switching from passive compliance with sin to a race that now requires you to go against it. As the author of Hebrews puts it: "Let us lay aside every weight, and the sin which so easily ensnares us, and let us run with endurance the race that is set before us" (12:1).

And again, Paul comments: "Do you not know that those who run in a race all run, but one receives the prize? Run in such a way that you may obtain it. And everyone who competes for the prize is temperate in all things" (1 Corinthians 9:24–25).

Temperate in all things—as in self-controlled, consistent. That's an athlete's mind-set. If you've been out of shape by letting a behavior rule you, then you, and *it*, will get used to it being in charge. But now you're going to reject its authority in your life, which is like booting out a dictator. (Hint: those guys don't go down easily.) So naturally, things will get a little rough when you play The Game.

Now, in playing, you have five primary goals:

1. To abstain from the sexual sin that's dominated you
2. To repair damaged relationships and make restitution
3. To maintain a permanent structure of discipline and accountability
4. To successfully manage sexual temptations when they arise
5. To correct unhealthy ways of relating

These are the goals we'll refer to throughout this book. Attain them, and you've won The Game. But as you can see, these are goals you not only attain but maintain as well. So you're a player not just for the next thirty days but for life. It is, after all, a lifestyle change you're looking for. You'll attain it in one month by following The Game Plan; you'll maintain it for life by incorporating this plan daily.

Isn't This Struggle Too Serious to Be Called a Game?

I guess using the term *game* does require an explanation, so let's step back and look at the broader picture to see where the idea of a game fits into it.

When we talk about growing beyond sin, we're really talking about the biblical concept of sanctification. After being born again, or saved, we're continually, by the Spirit of God, being transformed into more Christlike men: "But we all, with open face beholding as in a glass the glory of the Lord, are changed into the same image from glory to glory, even as by the Spirit of the Lord" (2 Corinthians 3:18 KJV).

We're also talking about spiritual warfare, mortification of the flesh, trials, temptations, and God's chastening, all of which are guaranteed in Scripture as part of the Christian life. We don't normally think of them as games. They're hard, at times, and serious.

But to call something a game doesn't necessarily make light of it. In his letter to Corinth, when Paul compared Christian living to the masteries, he was referring to a series of contests that were technically games but were, in fact, taken very seriously by the culture they were played in. Jamieson, Fausset, and Brown, in their excellent *Commentary on the Whole Bible*, have this to say about the games Paul referred to: "The Isthmian games were of course well known, and a subject of patriotic pride to the Corinthians, who lived in the immediate neighborhood. These periodical games were to the Greeks rather a passion than a mere amusement: hence their suitableness as an image of Christian earnestness."[1]

Sanctification and the overcoming of sin can be viewed as negative, dreary aspects of Christian living. But I'd rather see them the way Paul did: as challenging and, at times, even exciting. And as a passion, like the commentators said, not just an amusement. So to me, the term *game* is an upbeat, masculine, and accurate way of viewing what you're trying to do as a man who wants to live a better life. It's a war, certainly; a heartache, frequently. But it's also a noble contest, a race we're encouraged to run, and a game we're privileged to play. So I hope you'll find the concept of The Game to be both acceptable and helpful.

PLAYING THE GAME: THE PROCESS AND THE PLAN

When you play The Game, you go through a five-part process I call ROUTE: repentance, order, understanding, training, and endurance. These phases make up the main sections of this book, and three chapters will be devoted to each phase.

That means, once you begin The Game, you'll have fifteen chapters to read. I'm going to ask you to read one chapter every other day, which shouldn't be hard, since these chapters aren't long or technical. In each chapter you'll find ideas to learn and absorb as you read. Then the next day, after reading a chapter, you're going to follow the steps outlined in the action plan that follows each chapter. In other words, every other day you'll read one chapter, and every alternate day you'll take the steps listed in the action plan that come after each chapter you read. (To make it easier, I've labeled each chapter and action plan with Day 1, Day 2, etc., so you'll always know which day you're on and which page you should be reading.)

It will take you exactly thirty days to complete The Game Plan. So before you begin, make sure you have adequate time during the next thirty days to follow this program. "Adequate time" means approximately thirty minutes a day—a half-hour to read a chapter or, on the alternate days, a half-hour to complete the assignment—so plan your schedule accordingly before you start. Block out thirty minutes a day, preferably at the same time for continuity's sake. And please try not to skip a day. You'll build momentum and get better results if you stick to The Game Plan as it's written.

So Where Will All This Get Me?

I asked the same question when I began seeing a Christian counselor shortly after my own repentance in 1984. I wanted results and change, but I hadn't a clue how they were going to happen. So during our first session, my counselor briefed me on what I could expect by promising me six things. I still have the notes I took that day, and they go something like this:

1. You'll get a better understanding of the impact your sexual behavior has had on you—on your mind, heart, and body—and on the people you love.

2. You'll develop a concise plan to follow to help you separate yourself from that behavior and *stay* separated from it.

3. You'll get a management plan to help you cope with the temptations that will return, a plan that will include a daily and weekly structure that you'll make a part of your life.

4. You'll get tools with which to rebuild whatever relationships have been damaged by your behavior, as well as tools you'll use to correct ongoing relational problems.

5. You'll learn techniques you can use when sexual temptations come.

6. You'll understand and deal with the pain in your life that may have made you more susceptible to sexual sin.

That's what you can realistically expect if you follow this plan. I trust that's what you want and that you're willing to put some work into it. What you bring to the table is your motivation, your willingness to invest a half-hour daily in this program, and enough humility to be teachable. Bring those, and this book will, by God's grace, bring the insight and the tools. It will be an honor partnering with you in this effort.

So welcome to The Game. Let's play.

BEFORE WE BEGIN

You'll be spending approximately thirty minutes a day, for the next thirty days, either reading a chapter of the book or doing the action plan every other day. On odd-numbered days, you'll be reading the chapter for that day. On even-numbered days, you'll be doing the action plan for that day.

On the action plan days, you'll need a notebook with lined paper and a pen. Mark the top of the page Day 2, Day 4, and so on. This will be your action plan workbook. Or, if you prefer, use a word processor on your computer to create your own action plan workbook. (I recommend this instead of a notebook, since it will probably be quicker and easier.) Then type in the directions the action plan is giving you and any of the assignments or information required by that day's action plan.

You'll also need a Bible, and be sure you have access to a telephone and to the Internet, because on some days your action plan will require you to look up local resources or make connections by phone.

Try, if possible, to do your reading and action plans at the same time each day, as this will help ensure continuity.

QUALITIES OF A PLAYER

- A Player is a follower of Jesus Christ, imperfect but committed, who recognizes the value of sexual purity and strives for it daily.

- A Player has had his conscience awakened to the seriousness of compromise, either by an internal or external crisis of truth.

- A Player has made conscious and practical efforts to separate himself from any activities, relationships, or circumstances that would constitute or induce a sexual compromise.

- A Player is a man of daily prayer, daily Scripture reading, daily recommitment to purity, and daily review of the factors that motivate and inspire him.

- A Player knows that to keep his integrity thriving he'll need the additional integrity of men who share his vision. He stays accountable on a weekly basis, allowing his allies to know his weaknesses, struggles, and victories.

- A Player comes clean about his failures and attempts to make restitution to those who have been injured by his behavior.

- A Player knows the adversarial nature of the arena he plays in and the tactics his opponent will use against him, and he stays prepared for both.

- A Player is a steward of his emotions, so he addresses them by attending to his wounds through honesty and forgiveness.

- A Player understands sexual temptation and stays prepared for it by refusing to entertain it when it arises.

- A Player resists sexual temptation through daily training and practical resistance techniques.

- A Player recognizes that his body is not his own and that he will someday answer to its Owner for the way he has managed it.

- A Player confronts, humbly but clearly when necessary, always with the goal of improving his relationships.

- A Player has in place a relapse contingency plan that he never intends to use.

- A Player pursues his passion and calling beyond sexual purity.

- A Player loves his Lord, knowing his love for Him is imperfect but growing daily, and he expresses that love through devotion and obedience.

REPENTANCE

Day 1 Recruitment:
Getting Back into the Game
*God calls us out of the behavior we've gotten
comfortable with and reminds us of the
potential we're blocking and the life we're
neglecting.*

Day 2 Action Plan for Recruitment

Day 3 Crisis: Truth Hurts
*God confronts us with the truth by allowing
an internal or external crisis to interrupt us
and to motivate us to change.*

Day 4 Action Plan for Crisis

Day 5 Separation: Making the Final Cut
*We reject the behavior that has disrupted our
lives by separating ourselves from it and, to the
best of our ability, removing the opportunity to
return to it.*

Day 6 Action Plan for Separation

O

U

T

E

DAY 1

RECRUITMENT: GETTING BACK INTO THE GAME

To join in what God is doing,
what adjustments must I make in my life?

—HENRY BLACKABY AND CLAUDE KING,
EXPERIENCING GOD

I loved Little League; I just didn't care for baseball. Hand-eye coordination didn't come naturally to me, and I've never been fast, so strikeouts and missed catches were a problem. I could manage a football pretty well, and I blocked and tackled better than most, but baseball eluded me. Still, there I was, season after season, wearing a Little League uniform.

That, I liked. I liked the status. I liked saying, "I'm a ballplayer." I loved the camaraderie of the team and the social privileges it brought. I liked everything about baseball, in fact, but the game itself.

So I made up my own. At each game I'd sleepwalk through the first half, strike out, flub catches, or get tagged. Then when the others in the lineup took over during the second half, I'd sit on the bench with a concealed comic book, sipping a soda and letting my mind wander. Disinterested in the real game, I had my own game going.

Until my coach intervened.

I was in the middle of a terrific *Green Lantern* story while ignoring, as usual, my teammates and the game, when my coach snatched me off the bench, pulled my astonished face within a fraction of his,

3

and said, "Dallas, nobody made you join this team. You wanna play, play. You don't wanna play? Then turn in the uniform and quit calling yourself a player. Because when you carry this team's name but don't really play, you let the rest of us down. So make a decision."

That's the day I got serious. And within weeks, as I played seriously rather than halfheartedly, the game took on a whole new meaning.

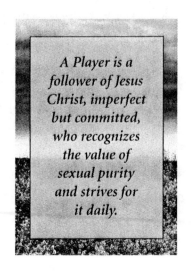

A Player is a follower of Jesus Christ, imperfect but committed, who recognizes the value of sexual purity and strives for it daily.

Don't Carry the Name If You Won't Play The Game

Christian men by the thousands are sitting on the bench, carrying the Name but ignoring The Game. And while there's no telling just how many believers have sexually compromised, the estimates aren't encouraging. More than 18 percent of the men polled in a Zogby/Focus on the Family survey, for example, identified themselves as Christians who used pornography.[2] Studies quoted in *Newsweek* magazine suggested that as many as 30 percent of the ministers interviewed had committed adultery,[3] and during an informal poll at the 1996 Promise Keepers men's conference, one out of three men admitted they "struggle with pornography."[4] James T. Draper Jr., the president of LifeWay Christian Resources, in fact, has gone so far as to say "it appears the sin of choice among Christians today is pornography."[5]

In other words, there are plenty of guys out there wearing the Christian uniform, calling themselves players but not truly and consistently playing The Game. If you're one of these guys and you're still looking for reasons, I want to offer you three.

YOUR MOST IMPORTANT
RELATIONSHIPS ARE SUFFERING

I liked my Little League coach. Truth to tell, I loved him. He was tough, funny, and dedicated; and like all good coaches, he loved his team by pushing them. But the more I slacked off on the field, the more I withdrew from him. It was especially hard looking him in the eye during practice, because his eyes were full of delighted pride when they looked at my hardworking teammates but full of irritation and disappointment when they rested on me. He knew I was failing, I knew that he knew, and our coach/player bond was polluted by that mutual knowledge.

My unwillingness to put effort into the game ruined my relationship with my coach, so I ducked him whenever possible.

I wasn't too fond of my teammates, either, because I knew I was letting them down. Have you noticed that when we know we're wronging another person but not willing to make it right, we tend to resent that person? I've seen this time and again in my married clients, for example, who know they're cheating on their wives via pornography or adultery. They're guilty, and the wife is the focal point of the guilt. But rather than deal with it, they avoid her and resent her for being a reminder of their sin.

My primary relationships suffered. Yours do too. You may belong to God. But something's missing, because you know that He knows there's compromise in your life, and the Father/son bond is polluted by that mutual knowledge.

Perhaps you're avoiding Him?

No surprise there. Man's first response to sin, after all, was to run away and hide from God, rather than run *to* Him for help. When Adam sinned, he fled the scene, making an insane attempt to duck God. And to my thinking, there's no sadder line in all of Scripture than God's heartbroken call to His rebel son: "Adam, where *are* you?"

Stop right there. Write your name in the blank in this sentence:

"_____, where *are* you?"

Read the sentence out loud with your name in it. Hear God saying it to you. Do this a couple of times. Can't you sense a Father's heart, angry and hurt, trying to get His beloved son to emerge from the bushes, discard those pathetic fig leaves (which aren't covering anything, anyway), and deal with the problem?

Of course, your relationships with others are suffering too. Secrecy does that, and if you've been entertaining a sexual sin, don't tell me you haven't become a pro at the secrecy game. You have to, in order to keep sexual sin alive. You have to do it secretly, then cover it up, lie about it, and pretend it isn't there. And the ongoing cover-up can't help but erect a wall of secrecy between you and the people who love you the most.

Close friendships and family relations suffer when a man leads a double life. Something dark and more than a little frightening happens to a guy like that. He's ashamed but not ready to admit the cause of his shame. So it poisons him, leaving him defensive, isolated, and spiritually dulled.

Yet all the while he may still function as a husband, parent, friend, church member, and brother. He may, in fact, have many good qualities and gifts; he's often (in my experience) likable and productive, even as his primary relationships suffer.

He's not a bad man. He's just not nearly the man he *could* be.

YOU'RE BEING GRATIFIED, PERHAPS, BUT NOT REALLY SATISFIED

Gratification is immediate and short-lived. Satisfaction, even when it requires gratification delay, is a long-term payoff.

Compare this to the difference between hunger and appetite, and I think you'll see what I mean. When your body requires food, it creates hunger pangs to satisfy that need. The hunger message is honest; it tells you what your body really needs, and when you respond by eating, you satisfy its requirements.

But along with your natural hunger, you may have also developed a large appetite, which is a desire for certain types and portions of food. If you overeat, that's usually why—your appetite claimed you needed more food (and probably food of a different sort) than your body required.

Appetite is dishonest in two ways. First, it disguises itself as hunger by saying, "I need," when a more honest statement would be, "I want." If you don't indulge your appetite, you'll find you can do with much less food than it demands.

Second, appetite often demands the sort of food you really don't need. Haven't you noticed that when your appetite is up, it usually doesn't call for broccoli? Mine sure doesn't. It wants cake, milk-shakes, and barrels of red meat. In other words, it craves *gratification*—the quick intensity of rich foods in large quantities—rather than the foods my body needs to truly *satisfy* it.

Let's take this idea further. When you go for gratification rather than satisfaction, you pig out. Since no one loves pigging out more than I do, I understand the joy of stuffing, chugging, and munching on foods rich in grease, fats, and starches. It's so gratifying—so immediate and intense. And for the moment, I'm a happy man.

But the happiness soon gives way to any number of discomforts: digestive problems, sluggishness, shame over my gluttony, and a general sense of being a loser who can't control himself. Only then do I realize (for the thousandth time!) I've sacrificed hours of satisfaction for a few minutes of indulgence.

When I diet successfully, though, I delay gratification and learn to eat what my body really *needs*. For the moment, yes, I'm a bit uncomfortable when I choose the salad over the burger. But when I delay gratification, the discomfort soon gives way to enhanced physical performance, higher energy, heightened self-respect, and the peace of being a man who takes care of himself properly. And I realize, gratefully, that this time I did it right. I earned hours of true satisfaction by sacrificing minutes of gratification.

When you sexually sin, you're gratifying an appetite that is inherently dishonest. It convinces you that what you *want*—the porn, the adultery, the hooker, the ritual—is, in fact, a *need*. And who can deny there's immediate impact when you say yes to that want? Intense sex can be amazing, all-encompassing, and utterly gratifying.

It soon shows itself, though, to be the sensual counterpart to pigging out, as pleasure gives way to discomfort—shame, disgust, guilt, fear of consequence, decreased self-respect, spiritual sluggishness, lost money, wasted time, broken promises, and perhaps even the general sense of being a loser who can't control himself. Only then might you realize you've sacrificed hours of emotional, mental, and spiritual satisfaction for a few minutes of indulgence.

There's a good reason for that. Let's look at the eating example again. Your body can only be satisfied, in the truest sense, when you fuel it properly. Even if you crave certain unhealthy foods, if they're not what your body is built for, then they'll eventually bring you more discomfort than pleasure.

Likewise, if you've truly been born again, then you've received a new nature that can only be satisfied, in the truest sense, when you fuel it properly. Paul illustrated this to the Romans when he asked, rhetorically, "How shall we who died to sin live any longer in it?" (Romans 6:2).

Notice he's not just saying sin is wrong. He's also pointing out its futility by showing the general futility of doing anything that violates your nature, even though it's pleasurable. Because if an activity is against your true nature, it can *gratify* but never *satisfy*.

For that reason, you'll go on reaping any number of uncomfortable feelings when you sexually sin. Count on anxiety, depression, shame, irritability, or despair, and count on them growing with time. Get into The Game, though, and you'll regain the joyful energy you're craving.

YOU'RE NOT FULFILLING A PRIMARY FUNCTION

Maybe I exaggerated my lack of baseball skills. I wasn't *that* bad. Sometimes, I was even fair. And I did, after all, have a position to play.

You guessed it: right field. It's a lonely place, right field—the ball doesn't visit often, and many a boy has found it either a place of banishment or a haven for daydreaming. But at least I had a function on the team, however small. And I was expected to fulfill it, because the ball does make it into right field on occasion, and a missed high fly could translate into a home run.

So when I approached the game halfheartedly, I wronged my team in a number of ways. We lost points because of my errors, my indifference demoralized my teammates and discouraged them from trying, and my behavior told the fans (parents, mostly) who'd come to the game that I didn't care, so why should they? I encouraged the opposing team, of course, and robbed everyone involved by diverting the energy I should have invested in the game, and instead putting it into my comic-book ritual.

I had a primary function. Neglecting it meant consequences.

Have you thought lately about a primary function Jesus said you have—one you cannot, to my thinking, fulfill as long as you're involved in ongoing sexual sin? "You are the salt of the earth; but if the salt loses its flavor, how shall it be seasoned? It is then good for nothing but to be thrown out and trampled underfoot by men. You are the light of the world. A city that is set on a hill cannot be hidden" (Matthew 5:13–14).

He didn't invite you to be salt and light, nor did He ask you to consider it. He said that's what you are. That's your function, and moral compromise weakens your ability to fulfill it, just as surely as drunkenness would weaken an athlete's ability to run a race. When your ability to fulfill your role is weakened, we all suffer.

Let's get practical about this. Suppose a Christian employee works in an office cubicle near an attractive woman. She's heard the gospel before, considered it, and maybe even attended a few church services. But she's undecided and, thereby, unsaved.

The man has an opportunity, through conversation and example, either to strengthen or to weaken her regard for Christianity. If he flirts with her, or if she overhears him crack a dirty joke, or if he views porn on the job and she finds out about it, his credibility (and worse, the *gospel's* credibility) is snuffed out. His sexual sin made him unable to fulfill a primary function, and the ripple effect kicks in. The church suffers by losing yet another notch of credibility; the woman suffers (perhaps eternally, a terrible thing to consider) by continuing to live apart from Christ; and whoever else might have been impacted by either of their lives if their lives had taken a better course suffers as well.

It's not just about you. It never was. Someone else, directly or indirectly, is also affected by your compromise. Every time a Christian's secret sin is brought to light, people who already hold Christianity in contempt get fresh ammunition, the undecided are given yet another reason not to decide, and fellow believers are demoralized in their own efforts to be an effective influence. And even if your sin has not (yet) been brought to light, the thing itself can't help but weaken your zeal by polluting your mind and hardening your heart. In that case, you may be a true believer, but you're hardly one who's equipped for battle.

INTERVENTION IS INEVITABLE

Considering all this, is it any wonder your Coach is intervening? The desire you have to preserve your integrity, the fear you have of losing what you value, or the guilt, anxiety, or dissatisfaction you're feeling over the form and degree of sexual sin in your life—these are all signs of God's intervention. He's interrupting your life because something is wrong and needs to be made right.

But interruption and rejection are far from the same. My coach interrupted me, not because he was rejecting me; on the contrary, he knew I could do better, and he still wanted me on the team. He knew my potential, and he still had purposes in mind for me.

He pulled me up short, in other words, because he *wasn't* through with me.

Your Coach hasn't given up on you either. In fact, He probably has more confidence in your future than you do. But for now, something's holding you back.

Whatever that something is, you can be sure of this much:

1. It's hurting someone. It's hurting you, of course; and it's offending God, which is no small offense. But it's also hurting someone close to you—a wife, a friend, a child—who deserves better.

2. It gratifies, but your own history by now should prove it doesn't really satisfy.

3. It's keeping you from fulfilling your potential, calling, and role. And we're all suffering as a result.

So I trust you're ready to get pulled over, corrected, repaired, and rebuilt. Because The Game is still on, and we *do* need you to play.

DAY 2

ACTION PLAN FOR RECRUITMENT

KEY VERSE

They said to one another, "Why are we sitting here until we die?"

—2 KINGS 7:3

PRINCIPLE

Inaction is a killer. The men in 2 Kings knew they had a serious problem. Their problem had overtaken them and would eventually destroy them if they did nothing about it. So they asked themselves the question I hope you're asking yourself as well: "Why should I just sit here?"

ACTION

Write or type into your own computer the answers to the following questions.

1. We'll begin by assessing the problem. What specific sexual sin is causing a crisis in your life? It will most likely be one of the following:

internet pornography	adultery
video pornography	sex before marriage
pornographic magazines or books	homosexual sex
internet chat rooms	S and M
phone sex	cross-dressing
strip clubs/bars	massage parlors
prostitutes	voyeurism
anonymous encounters	one-night stands

2. Approximately how many years or months have you been engaging in this behavior? (If you're involved in more than one of the above, then list each one and the approximate time you've been involved in it.)

3. What effect has this behavior had on your relationship with God? After writing your answer, read it out loud twice.

4. What effect has this behavior had on your self-respect? After writing your answer, read it out loud twice.

5. If you're married or involved in a serious relationship with a woman, what effect has this behavior had on your relationship with your wife, fiancée, or girlfriend? (If you're single and unattached, skip this and move on.) After writing your answer, read it out loud twice.

6. If you're a father, how would your child/children be affected emotionally if they knew of your behavior? (If you're not a father, skip this and move on.) After writing your answer, read it out loud twice.

7. Why have you continued in this behavior? After writing your answer, read it out loud twice.

RATIONALE

Part of what gets you motivated to play The Game is the realization of what you're doing to yourself, the people you love, and your relationship with God when you *don't* play. So now's the time to assess your behavior and the impact it's having.

PRAYER
(Read this silently, then pray it aloud.)

Father, give me the courage and the integrity to face what I've wanted to avoid. Let me see clearly the damage my private pleasure has had on the most important parts of my life, and when I examine the effects of my sin, let that knowledge motivate me to do what's necessary. I ask this in Jesus's name. Amen.

DAY 3

CRISIS: TRUTH HURTS

Sometimes fear can be good. When you are afraid things are going to get worse if you don't do something, it can prompt you into action.

—SPENCER JOHNSON, MD, *WHO MOVED MY CHEESE?*

No pain, no gain—it's as true of sanctification as it is of athletics.

I learned a painful lesson about "loving interruption" when I was about four years old. My family's home sat on the eighteenth fairway of a private golf course, and the location was rugged and beautiful. The fairway was easy to reach from our backyard, and a few hundred yards away, a steep little road for golf carts plunged down to a suspended bridge overlooking the green. It was a sharp downhill path we walked frequently, but I wanted to give it a whirl on my little bicycle. Dad wouldn't hear of it—"Too steep, Joey; are you nuts? You could get killed!"—which only made me more determined to try it. It looked fun, I was already a hotshot on my two-wheeler, and what did Dad know, anyway? He saw danger; I saw a good time.

We were out on the fairway one evening, I on my bike and Dad walking alongside, when I begged him, for the hundredth time, to let me coast down the hill. He refused; I sulked. Then a neighbor approached us, Dad struck up a conversation with him, and I saw my chance. As soon as his back was turned, I shot off straight for the downhill road. My bike was just teetering over the edge when *wham!*—both it and I were slammed sideways onto the grass. Dad, quicker than I'd given him credit for, had sprinted toward me when he saw where I was headed, grabbed the back of my shirt just as I reached the hill, and jerked me over.

He interrupted me before I went any farther, because he knew the thrill I was after could kill me. Wouldn't any good father do the same?

A Loving "Halt!"

That divine interruption may explain why you feel such discomfort over this behavior. It may even seem that God is hounding you—which, of course, is true.

Or maybe, in your case, it answers another question: "Why did God allow me to get caught?"

Why, indeed? After all, you may have been getting away with this for years. So why now, all of a sudden, did your wife get the urge to check your computer history? Or why were you seen going into the topless bar? Or why did the affair come to light?

> *A Player has had his conscience awakened to the seriousness of compromise, either by an internal or external crisis of truth.*

You may think *punishment* is the answer, since punishment seems justified. So you figure He's just giving you a long overdue kick in the butt. You sinned; you're busted; you suffer. And that, you may think, is all there is to it.

But if that's your conclusion, you're underestimating both God's purposes and your potential. Divine interruption isn't punishment. It's an act of love to keep you from going any further in your error. And it's evidence of God's ongoing interest in you and your future.

"As many as I love," Jesus said, "I rebuke and chasten" (Revelation 3:19). And on the subject of chastening—as in *correcting*—the author of Hebrews points out: "But if you are without chastening, of which all have become partakers, then you are illegitimate and not sons" (12:8).

Look at it another way. When a racer's vehicle needs repair, he doesn't junk it. He pulls it over for a pit stop, and he certainly doesn't do that because he's finished with the vehicle. Just the opposite—he does it because he's *not* finished with it! It's a valuable car, and he has specific purposes in mind for it. After all, the pit stop isn't a junkyard but a place for repair and rebuilding.

When God interrupts you, He pulls you over for a pit stop. You're still a vehicle, your Driver has eternal purposes, and He's determined to see them fulfilled. So there's life after the pit stop.

Yes, it's a scary thing when your Father yanks you off your bike and lets your sin be found out. But it's scarier if He doesn't, because what would that say about you? If God isn't chastening you, then He isn't Fathering you; if He isn't Fathering you, then you don't belong to Him. So this isn't punishment; it's proof of ownership. And what often brings it about is a crisis of truth that generates unpleasant but necessary pain.

King David: Compromise, Crisis, Correction

No one illustrates this better than King David, who embodied the kind of greatness we'd love to achieve and the level of failure we pray we'll avoid. Looking at the harrowing episode in his life that included adultery and murder, you can see how the crisis of truth God sent him became his painful salvation.

I'm convinced David's tragedy began with a compromise much less notorious than the "big sin" that followed. We seldom consider it, yet it's plainly recorded in Scripture. David, a man after God's own heart, had sexually compromised decades before his most notorious transgression.

When he was anointed king of Israel at age thirty, the Law already made it plain what God expected of a king: "He shall not multiply horses for himself. . . . Neither shall he multiply wives for himself, lest his heart turn away; nor shall he greatly multiply silver and gold for himself" (Deuteronomy 17:16–17).

The standards were clear, and David complied—with most of

them. When he conquered the Moabites, for example, he destroyed their excess horses, in obedience to the command not to hoard them (1 Chronicles 18:4). And he dedicated the spoils of war—silver, gold, and brass—to God, rather than to himself, in deference to the command not to multiply riches (1 Chronicles 18:11). King David was exemplary in many ways, but he compromised in one—women.

David multiplied wives to himself, a direct violation of the Law (1 Chronicles 14:3). As we see from Scripture, David's life didn't fall apart the moment he compromised. In fact, an observer might have concluded that his compromise didn't matter much and was just a "blip" in an otherwise terrific life.

Could David himself have thought the same? It's easy to believe he did. I can imagine him considering his life as a young king, both the good parts and the compromised ones, and telling himself, "In many ways, I'm reigning successfully. My relationship with God is intact; my responsibilities are being fulfilled; the nation's doing well. So even if I have compromised in this one area, how bad can it be? It certainly isn't destroying me."

I wonder how much of yourself you can see in David at this point. Maybe you were already familiar with the Bible when you began, or continued, your private sexual vice. When you used the porn, flirted with the co-worker, or got on the chat room, you probably weren't ignorant of God's standards. You knew; still, you indulged.

But then again, can't you also point out other parts of your life—significant ones, at that—in which you obey God and follow His guidelines to the letter? There may be any number of good works you do within church and home, and other parts of your life may be as exemplary as David's. To a point, that's good, but it also creates a problem, because it's easier to minimize an ongoing sin in your life when you're living obediently in other areas.

What you may not realize is that, like David, your loss of control in that one area may set you up for an explosion that will overshadow all the other parts of your life.

David's later tragedy with Bathsheba, as chronicled in 2 Samuel 11–12, bears this out. He had reigned in Israel about twenty years by that time, was highly favored by God, and had a breathtaking résumé of spiritual and political triumphs. Yet one night, while Israel was at war and he'd stayed behind, he was strolling on his rooftop when he spied a beautiful woman bathing. The king saw, lusted, and obsessed. And the nightmare began.

He found out who she was, learned she was married to a man who was in battle at the time, sent for her anyway, and then took her. The lines were crossed quickly, impulsively, and you might even say effortlessly. It's striking how easily a good man slips into evil deeds. And there was, of course, worse to come.

The Compromise Brings On the Crisis of Truth

After his one-night stand with Bathsheba, David knew he'd done wrong, but nothing indicates he confessed it or, for that matter, even dealt with it. He knew what God's law said about his behavior, but he ignored the law and the behavior as well. But they couldn't be ignored for long.

Bathsheba sent word that she was pregnant, and David scrambled. As usual, the cover-up was worse than the sin. He tried to get her husband, Uriah, home from battle and into bed with his own wife—thinking, no doubt, that Uriah would have sex with her and assume *that* was the cause of her pregnancy. But Uriah refused marital privileges when his comrades were still in battle, and David, now panicking, graduated from weakness to evil. He arranged for Uriah to be put in the front lines of battle and thereby killed. Then, having committed adultery and murder, David tried putting it all behind him. Yet it refused to stay put, and a crisis of truth was in the making.

THE CRISIS OF TRUTH FIRST COMES FROM WITHIN

It began internally, as a crisis of conscience. Read again David's description in Psalm 32 of what life was like when he refused to confess—the aching bones, the sleeplessness—and you see a man with an internal crisis who is growing more uncomfortable by the minute. He knew the lines he'd crossed, and his conscience was responding. Still, he pushed it down, trying to ignore it and telling himself that he'd gotten away with it and that he should forget it and move on.

I can't help but wonder if you haven't done the same.

You may have crossed a line, like David did when he first took wives, and found (as he did) that the world didn't fall apart. Few men get caught the first time. Usually, they repeat whatever sexual activity they're into without consequence. Or, I should say, without *external* consequence. After all, there's really no such thing as "getting away" with sin. At the very least it hinders fellowship with God, hardens the heart, and pollutes the mind. Still, there's usually a period—a long one, sometimes—during which a man regularly indulges in sexual sin and seems to get away with it.

When that happens, it's not because God is ignoring the sin. He is, rather, giving the man what I call space for repentance. That's an undefined period in which God gives you room to take care of the problem before the problem overwhelms you.

If you've been given space to repent, you'll do one of two things: you'll either use it wisely by taking action while you can, or you'll make the common mistake of mistaking space for repentance as permission to continue. That's easy to do, because we tend to be consequence-driven. When we get away with something once, we're inclined to think we'll get away with it indefinitely.

THE CRISIS OF TRUTH MAY GO
FROM THE INTERNAL TO THE EXTERNAL

David must have thought he'd gotten away with it. Months went by while he kept his sin hidden. Notice, too, that even before his adultery and murder, he'd ignored both his conscience and God's law for years. Not entirely, of course, but just enough to have set himself up for calamity. Still, he seems to have concluded it was behind him, until the crisis of truth went from the internal to the external, and he was confronted by the prophet Nathan.

Nathan began by telling David a story about a man who'd done something similar to what David had done. David, not recognizing himself in the story yet hating the sin the man in the story committed, reacted strongly, commanding the man be put to death. With that, Nathan sledgehammered David with an external crisis of truth: "You are the man" (2 Samuel 12:7).

You'll be reading the detailed account of this conversation in Day 4, but for now, let me paraphrase. In one excruciating confrontation, Nathan drives the horrible truth home:

You are exactly the person you say you hate.
You have been given so much, yet you've despised it.
You are an adulterer.
You are a murderer.
You have created human misery.
You have caused unbelievers to commit blasphemy.
You are not the man you think you are!

King David—a good man who'd done evil things in secret that were now being published openly—crumpled under the weight of the truth. The wrong he'd done but had refused to face was spelled out brutally and would no longer be ignored. The pain David felt, though necessary, must have been indescribable. Yet the wound Nathan inflicted was the terrible and liberating truth.

THE CRISIS OF TRUTH INFLICTS A WOUND

The Wound is the trauma a man feels when he sees both what he's done and the damage he's done. The Wound is hard, but it's necessary for recovery. Because to truly recover, we need to see that, to some extent, we've been kidding ourselves.

Look at Peter. He thought he was braver than the other disciples and, I suppose, more committed. So when Jesus warned that all of them would forsake Him under pressure, Peter separated himself from the others and said, in essence, "*These* guys might wimp out when it gets tough, but me? Never!" He then suffered The Wound when he realized, after denying Christ, he wasn't nearly as brave and committed as he thought he was.

Then there's Job. He complained about the unfairness of his trials, arguing his own righteousness and saying, in essence, "I'm too good of a man to have to go through this!" A thorough dressing-down from God Himself followed, and Job came to a shattering realization: his "perfection" was a myth. The Wound hit him so hard, in fact, he went from promoting his goodness to uttering, "I abhor myself" (Job 42:6).

That's The Wound. You feel it when you realize you're not the man you thought you were, and it's been experienced by countless others during their own turning points.

It does have its purpose, because you're not likely to give up sexual sin until you see its seriousness. That means facing things you've probably avoided. But when you do, you experience one of three things that are needed, in my opinion, for true repentance: you get scared, sad, or angry—all of which are emotions that will, I hope, become motivators.

David experienced, I think, all three. He was heartbroken over his behavior, angry with himself, and frightened of the consequences. And that powerful combination of emotions drove him to humility, prayer, and necessary action. His crisis of truth was not, in other words, the end. It was the beginning of repentance and restoration. God certainly didn't send Nathan to confront him because his life was *over*, but because He wanted it to be *better*. In *David: A Man of Passion and Destiny*, author Chuck Swindoll puts it well: "Why did such a major change take place in David's life and attitude? First, because David hurt enough to admit his need."[6]

Shame, outrage, fear—they seem like negative emotions, but they also produce enough discomfort and energy to shake a man out of his complacency and into redemptive action. They help get him into The Game.

So today, you share David's wound and the painful self-awareness it brings. Then, admitting your need, you move toward repentance, which is the beginning of true recovery.

Day 4

ACTION PLAN FOR CRISIS

Key Verse

You are the man.

—2 Samuel 12:7

Principle

God still loved David very much and had a future for him. But there was no way the king could move on in life until he faced what he'd been hiding. That meant facing himself and how far he'd fallen from the man he used to be. (And the man he *still* could be!)

You need to see yourself in this story—a man beloved of God with potential and a future, but one whose compromise has to be dealt with before he can move on. To deal with it, you need to see the contrast between what you've allowed yourself to be versus what you can still become.

Action

1. Read 2 Samuel 11 (the entire chapter) and 12:1–9. Notice not only David's downward spiral (from lust to adultery, from adultery to covering up, from covering up to murder), but also how he seemed to try putting it behind him without confessing and dealing with it. Notice, too, the crisis of truth God sent through Nathan.

2. Write or type whatever ways you've tried to hide or cover up your sin. What effect has this "covering up" had on your mind and on your confidence in general?

3. How do you think God has been trying to draw your attention to this behavior (conscience, conviction of the Holy Spirit, circumstances, etc.)?

4. Take a few minutes to become your own Nathan. Look at the following list of things a man does when he deliberately continues in sexual sin, then read this list out loud to yourself. Think carefully about what you're reading.

I've deliberately put my pleasure before God.
I've ignored the grief I've been inflicting on Him.
I've polluted my own body and mind.
I've wasted precious time and energy on a selfish indulgence.
I've crippled my ability to be salt and light in a world that needs both.
I've let people down even if they're unaware of it.
I've participated in the sort of evil I say I'm against.
I've lied, pretended, and kept up a false front.
I've broken promises and commitments.
I've not had the courage to come clean and deal with this.
I'm not the man others think I am.
I'm not the man I could be.

RATIONALE

Godly sorrow over sin is the gateway to true repentance; true repentance is the gateway to true change. You won't experience godly sorrow, though, until you've let the impact of your behavior sink in. That's the reason The Wound is so crucial to The Game.

PRAYER

Father, open my eyes to both the seriousness of my behavior and to Your stubborn love for me, which refuses to let me settle for anything less than Your best. Help me to both grieve my sin and to keep from being swallowed up in grief. Give me the sensitivity to weep over my wrongdoing; give me the faith to believe You point out my problem so it can be solved. Protect me from self-condemnation, but do not shield me from self-awareness. I ask this in Jesus's name. Amen.

DAY 5

SEPARATION: MAKING THE FINAL CUT

These petty toys, my longtime fascinations,
still held me. They plucked at the garment of my flesh,
and murmured caressingly, "Dost thou cast us off?
From this moment on, shall this delight be
unlawful to thee forever? Dost thou think thou
canst live without these things?"

—St. Augustine

Sometimes walking away from a pet sin means saying a necessary but very difficult good-bye.

The day I decided to get back into The Game, I learned what deep friendships I'd developed with those "petty toys" St. Augustine referred to. When I cleaned out my closet full of pornography, cancelled the Playboy Channel on my cable service, and burned the phone numbers of contacts I knew I had to sever, I felt tremendous relief.

For a day.

Then it became clear to me, the next morning, that something was missing. I was used to an early "shot" of porn to help rouse me for the day; my wind-down time before bed always included either an X-rated video or, at least, a glimpse of the Playboy Channel. All gone, and now my apartment seemed suddenly empty and tomb-like. I began feeling, in fact, a ridiculous sort of remorse over having abandoned my "friends"—the videos, magazines, and cable shows

26

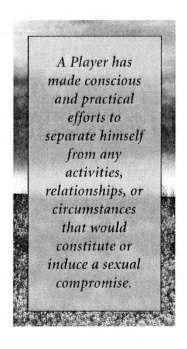

A Player has made conscious and practical efforts to separate himself from any activities, relationships, or circumstances that would constitute or induce a sexual compromise.

that had faithfully kept me company whenever I needed them. Twenty-four hours after throwing them out, I began wondering how, after all the years we'd been together, I was going to function without them.

"This is absurd!" I told myself. "I've done the right thing, God will honor it, and where did that stuff ever get me, anyway?"

But try as I might, I couldn't entirely push a very unwanted thought away: *I miss my friends, I miss my friends . . .*

Still, I'd done what I could, for now. Repentance is, after all, about *action*, not just *emotion*. It's something you do.

GAME STATUS

By now, you should have

- Identified the behavior you need to stop now and resist in the future
- Examined its effect on you and your loved ones
- Seen the contrast between it and your better ideals and beliefs
- Felt something in response to this self-examination

This, in turn, creates the repentant mind-set. Repentance, you remember, is the first part of the five-phase recovery process of ROUTE: repentance, order, understanding, training, and endurance. And that, to my thinking, is what recovery is about.

So now you're getting out onto the field, playing in earnest. Because now you separate yourself, once and for all, from the behavior you know you can't continue.

BEGIN THE GAME WITH CONFIDENCE

Remember, your recovery was God's idea, not yours. *He* thought this up and then woke you up so you'd get with the program.

Paul told the Philippians, "It is God who works in you both to will and to do for His good pleasure" (2:13). So even your desire to abandon sin comes from Him.

He's also the One who sustains your recovery. Certainly, human effort is involved, which we'll look at more fully on Day 19. But David, who knew something about correction and recovery, summed the process up well: "The LORD will perfect that which concerns me; Your mercy, O LORD, endures forever; do not forsake the works of Your hands" (Psalm 138:8).

God not only began this process in you, but He will sustain it, even when you're discouraged and ready to throw in the towel. You are, after all, the work of His hands. Feel free to remind Him of that (as if He'd forget!), just as David did. When you do, you're really reminding yourself.

And of course, what God begins, He completes. The apostle Paul assured the Philippians that he was "confident of this very thing, that He who has begun a good work in you will complete it until the day of Jesus Christ" (1:6).

Have you ever watched a terrific thriller and agonized along with the leading man when he goes through incredible ups and downs? I have, and I've screamed at the screen when things get tense: "Don't trust that woman! Don't go through that door! Turn around, quick! He's got a gun!"

I like to get into it. Then, if I really enjoyed the thriller, I'll rent it when it comes out on DVD. I notice that, when I view it a second time, I can enjoy it in ways I couldn't the first time. Once I know the ending (assuming it's a happy one), I can relax and appreciate the direction, scenery, and orchestral score. I can even enjoy the tense moments, because I've seen the end, and I know it'll be OK.

Likewise, God has seen the end of your movie. He sees you completed, seated at His right hand, game over, victory won. So while it's true you can grieve, anger, or offend Him, you're not *worrying* Him. What He began, He'll complete.

REPENTANCE EQUALS REJECTION THROUGH SEPARATION

So what does repentance look like? When you repent, you reject a behavior by separating yourself from it. That's the acid test of true repentance.

If you've been using Internet pornography, for example, you'll separate yourself from it by any means necessary. You'll either get a filter or a new service provider, or you'll give your password to someone who can log you in and monitor your on-line activities. Or, if all else fails, you'll get rid of the Internet altogether. (The Day 6 action plan will cover this in more detail.)

If you've been involved in an adulterous relationship, you'll separate yourself from the other person by severing communication. Or if you've been into commercial sex—prostitutes, strip bars, massage parlors—you'll avoid the areas where those services are available. If you've been having sex with your girlfriend, you and she will commit to never being alone together in a place where sex would be possible. In all cases, the overriding principle is this: find practical ways to separate yourself from the acting out and from whatever draws you back into it.

STAY PREPARED

But repentance isn't just about separation. It's about preparation as well—preparation against the temptation to return to the behavior you've rejected.

That sounds cynical, doesn't it? After all, if you've had a crisis of truth over your sin, then surely (you would think) that sin would be the last thing you'd ever think of returning to!

And sure—for a time the thought of it may be repulsive. But you and I have a problem we may as well face: any experience we've found pleasurable or meaningful has been recorded—deeply and graphically—in our brains, where it's filed away for future reference. So what the heart rejects, the brain still stores up in its memory banks.

The sin you've rejected today may appeal to you tomorrow because, unfortunately, it's always available. So let me encourage you to assume that, no matter how sincere your repentance is, at some point you'll be tempted to return to the behavior you've rejected.

Even the apostle Paul kept himself prepared and admitted, "I discipline my body and bring it into subjection, lest, when I have preached to others, I myself should become disqualified" (1 Corinthians 9:27).

Paul was inarguably a new creation: an apostle, teacher, and evangelist. But he didn't see himself as being above the pull of temptation. He stayed prepared, and like a boxer who knows he might be challenged at any time, he stayed in fighting trim. So if Paul recognized the power of temptation and stayed prepared for it, then you and I don't dare do any less.

OK, by now you know what you need to do, and you'll begin doing it tomorrow. You're in the repentance phase of The Game, which is a time for planning and taking action. So tomorrow's action plan will spell out the specifics of your repentance and offer you a framework for accomplishing your goals. But before we stop for today, I'd like you to consider something.

Paul began his letter to the Ephesians by saying, "He chose us in Him before the foundation of the world, that we should be holy and without blame before Him in love" (1:4).

Don't end this chapter without giving his words some thought. Before the world was created, God saw you and said, "Yes. This is My man. I take into account everything he'll do, both good and evil, and I still say yes, he's Mine."

You were known and chosen centuries before you were born, and you were chosen with a purpose: to be holy and blameless before Him. No point in trying to figure that out—you might as well just enjoy it. There's an ancient agenda at work in your repentance, a plan that was set in motion before you had anything to say about it.

To repent, then, is to enter into the purposes and future God has for you.

No wonder you're in The Game. It's your destiny.

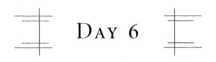

DAY 6

ACTION PLAN FOR SEPARATION

KEY VERSE

If your right eye causes you to sin, pluck it out and cast it from you; for it is more profitable for you that one of your members perish, than for your whole body to be cast into hell. And if your right hand causes you to sin, cut it off and cast it from you; for it is more profitable for you that one of your members perish, than for your whole body to be cast into hell.

—MATTHEW 5:29–30

PRINCIPLE

When you repent of a behavior, you reject it by separating yourself from it. If the behavior hasn't been rejected, it hasn't been repented of. And without repentance, nothing changes. So now is when you begin playing The Game in earnest. You're on the field now, taking concrete action to separate yourself from the behavior you're rejecting.

ACTION

All sexual sins require immediate action, but the action for each will be different. As a rule, you identify the behavior and do the following:

1. Prayerfully renounce the behavior, commit to abstaining from it, and pray for the strength to keep that commitment.

A sample prayer would be: *Lord, I renounce and reject this activity as being abominable to You, hurtful to those I love, and demeaning and destructive to me. I turn from it with my whole heart and am determined never to repeat it. But I need Your strength, power, and grace to keep this commitment, and I ask for all three.*

2. Take *immediate* action when necessary.

3. Take *preventive* action through accountability.

To help get you started, here are some examples of immediate actions you can take for some behaviors and preventive actions you can take for others.

IF YOU'VE BEEN USING INTERNET PORNOGRAPHY

Goal: Abstain from porn use by removing access to the porn.

Method: If you're going to keep the Internet in your home, then you need an Internet filter to block out porn, a new Internet service provider (ISP) that excludes porn, or an on-line accountability system. To help you decide which is best for you, log on to these two sites, both of which compare different Internet filtering and software devices:

www.smartcomparisons.com
www.internet-filter-review.toptenreviews.com

These will help you see what's available and which type of device suits your needs. Only you can decide, but let me give you a few hints.

If you're computer savvy, you probably need a new ISP rather than a blocking device. Guys who are proficient with computers report that it's fairly easy to get around these devices if you know the system. So look for a new service provider, not just a blocking filter, if you're good on computers.

The on-line accountability option is especially good, since it lets someone else view your on-line history and increases accountability.

The downside is that this option may or may not include blocking or filtering.

Nothing is 100 percent foolproof. Your goal is not to make it *impossible* to use on-line porn. The goal is to make it harder and therefore less likely.

I would also personally recommend these on-line products, as I've either used them myself, or they've been repeatedly endorsed by my clients who've used them:

www.purerestoration.com
www.internetfilters.net
www.afafilter.com

If, however, you've tried filters and other on-line devices in the past without success, now's the time to ask yourself (and be brutally honest, please) whether or not you really need the Internet. Most of us could survive without it. If it continues to trip you up, then, as Jesus said, it's better to go through the inconvenience of doing without it than to continue in a behavior that's destroying you. There's the choice: inconvenience or destruction. For that reason, you may decide to discontinue the Internet altogether.

But if for business reasons you really can't do without the Internet and filtering devices don't work for you, then consider giving someone else (wife, close friend, family member) the password to your computer and letting them question you each time you use it. This is, of course, an extra hassle. And that may be just what you need.

Another option—do without the Internet in your home, but when you need it, use your local library or a copy store, where you're less likely to view pornography.

IF YOU'VE BEEN WATCHING PORN ON TELEVISION
Goal: Abstain from porn by removing access.

Method: Call your cable service now, and have it turned off immediately or order one that doesn't include porn. (And by porn, I mean either hard-core or so-called soft-core like the Playboy

Channel.) Be sure your service also doesn't offer HBO, Showtime, or Cinemax, as these channels regularly feature pornographic material, no matter what else they may call it.

If you can't find another cable service that does *not* offer these channels, then do without cable. Believe me, you can, and you've got to. If you've been watching porn on TV, and if you continue to make those channels available, you will definitely watch it again.

IF YOU HAVE PORNOGRAPHIC MATERIAL
IN YOUR HOME, CAR, OR PLACE OF BUSINESS

Goal: Abstain from porn use by getting rid of it and by setting up accountability to help keep you from using it in the future.

Method: Gather it now, bag it, and trash it at a location separate from your home (preferably a Dumpster or the type of receptacle where no one else is likely to see or pick up the materials).

When we get to Days 9 and 10, you'll set up an accountability network to help keep you from buying and using porn in the future. For now, after throwing the materials out, take a minute to pray in your home that God would cleanse the environment that has been polluted and make your home a place that honors Him.

Here's a sample prayer: *Forgive me, Lord, for defiling this home You gave me. I renounce the sexual idols I took in and all they stand for. Replace their pollution with Your peace, and make this place a sanctuary that honors You in all ways. Amen.*

IF YOU'VE BEEN IN AN ADULTEROUS RELATIONSHIP

Goal: Terminate the relationship; abstain from future contact; rebuild your marriage.

Method: You need to notify the other party as soon as possible and explain why you need to break this off. Decide now what day (again, as soon as possible!) and time you're going to do this, and plan your schedule accordingly.

This will obviously be complicated and emotionally draining, so let me offer you some steps to take.

First, let someone close to you—a pastor, friend, or family member—know what you're planning to do. You'll do better if you know someone is rooting for you and supporting you through the process. Tell this person specifically when, where, and how you're going to break off the relationship. Tell him your fears and concerns, and then get his feedback and, hopefully, his encouragement.

Let him know the specific day and time you're breaking it off, then ask him if you can call him afterward for some debriefing and prayer.

Here's a sample way to approach your friend: "I've got to tell you something difficult, and I'm going to need your honesty and your support. I've gotten involved with someone, and I know it's got to end. I'm planning to break it off tomorrow afternoon, and here's what I'm planning to tell her. [Then tell him whatever you've decided to say.] What do you think? Any suggestions? I'm telling her at four o'clock—please remember me then. And can I call you after I talk to her? It would be good to debrief with you. Thanks for being the kind of friend I need at a time like this."

Second, prepare the main points you want to make to the other party when breaking it off. They should include

- A firm statement that the relationship is wrong and has to end now

- A clear apology for allowing it, and a recognition of your responsibility for the relationship and for allowing it to continue

- A clear statement that from now on the two of you will not be communicating for any reason

Before actually doing this, be sure to read "Marriage" in the appendix. It will go over the basics: what to say, what not to say, how to come clean with your wife, and what to expect as you restore your marriage.

IF YOU'VE BEEN HAVING SEX
WITH YOUR GIRLFRIEND OR FIANCÉE

Goal: Restore integrity to the relationship by abstaining from sex.

Method: Contact her today and let her know your commitment to being a more responsible leader in the relationship. Make a mutual covenant that you will only be together when and where it would be impossible to have sex and that you'll avoid being alone together at any other time.

Please don't kid yourself about this. Once you've bonded sexually, you're likely to continue having sex, no matter how much you want to stop. You've bonded, and the bonding works like superglue. So rather than trust your own efforts and discipline, assume you *will* have sex if you're *able* to have sex. And that, of course, means only being together in situations where you're not able to do so.

That won't kill the romance in your relationship, by the way. You can still enjoy romantic dinners, movies, plays, concerts, and virtually any kind of party or group activity. You only need to avoid being alone together in a place where sex would be possible. If you're serious about your relationship and you want to build a future based on mutual trust and respect, then this isn't asking much.

IF YOU'VE BEEN USING PROSTITUTES

Goal: Abstain from future use by avoidance and accountability.

Method: Make an appointment today with either your doctor or your local county health facility to be tested for HIV or for other sexually transmitted diseases. This is crucial, no matter what specific sex acts you have or haven't engaged in with the prostitute(s). As a steward of your body, you have the responsibility to know your medical status. This is doubly true, of course, if you're married.

Make a commitment to avoid driving past the area you would normally meet prostitutes. Being in proximity to that area will trigger old desires and make it harder to abstain.

I think you can see how to take the necessary actions. Begin with a specific prayer; then, if immediate action is called for and possible, take it. Otherwise, you'll be taking preventive action when you get your accountability structure set up.

No matter what behavior it is you're turning from, write down or type into your computer the following information:

1. Name the "benefits" you've been getting from your sexual sin—that is, what you've been getting out of this behavior. This is a way of counting the cost involved in giving it up. There are usually several "benefits"; here are some of the most common:

   - It comforts me
   - I get affection from this
   - I get affirmation from this
   - It kills my pain
   - I feel an emotional connection.
   - It's exciting.
   - It makes me feel powerful.
   - It distracts me when I'm bored.

   If any of these apply, list them. But also ask yourself: "What else have I been getting out of this?"

2. What will your life be like five years from now if you don't turn away from this behavior? Specifically, what will your frame of mind be like, what will your marriage be like, what will your spiritual life be like, and what impact will this behavior have on your job, career, ministry, and reputation five years from now, if current trends continue?

RATIONALE

By counting the cost of giving up this behavior, then weighing its benefits against its liabilities, you make a reasoned commitment to both reject it and abstain from it.

PRAYER

Lord, in leaving this behavior or relationship, I feel as though I'm walking away from an old, reliable friend. This sin has offended and grieved You, and it has damaged me and all I hold dear. But it has been a part of me so long I feel, even as I reject it, that I'm cutting off a part of myself. Help me to see sin for what it is, in all its horribleness, and keep me from being dazzled by its memory and attractiveness in the future.

Three things I need from You if I'm to follow You in this way:

1. *I need Your strength and courage to follow through on the commitment I'm making today.*

2. *I need Your wisdom as I deal with the specifics and details involved in turning from this behavior.*

3. *I need deeper faith in You and in Your ability to keep me from returning to the very thing I'm now rejecting.*

Please help me to be the good and faithful servant You've called me to be by giving me all three. I ask this in Jesus's name. Amen.

GAME STATUS UPON COMPLETION
OF SECTION ONE

By the end of Section One (Repentance), you should have done the following: (Check off each item you've completed.)

_____ Named the sexual behavior or behaviors that have disrupted your life and that you're ready to abandon.

_____ Identified the effects this behavior has had on your relationship with God, your closest relationships with family and friends, and on your relationship with yourself.

_____ Taken practical and verifiable steps to separate yourself from this behavior. (Acid test: if you were on trial for repenting of this behavior, would there be enough evidence of your repentance to convict you?)

_____ Told at least one trusted friend about the sin you're rejecting and the actions you've taken to reject it. (Sample message to friend: "I'm going to trust you enough to tell you something embarrassing but important. I've been using pornography for years, but I'm finally doing something about it. I've thrown out the porn and gotten a filter on my computer. I don't want to keep this a secret any longer, and that's why I'm telling you. Please pray that I'll have the strength and integrity to stay clean.")

If you've left any of these action items undone, go back and complete them before continuing to Section Two.

SECTION TWO

R

Day 7   **Structure: Your Daily Meds**
*We establish a set of daily disciplines and
incorporate them as part of a lifestyle change.*

ORDER

Day 8   **Action Plan for Structure**

Day 9   **Alignment: Teammates and Allies**
*We develop relationships with mentors,
accountability allies, and friends who share
our vision.*

Day 10   **Action Plan for Alignment**

Day 11   **Confession and Restitution**
*We make confession and attempt restitution
with those who have been directly impacted
by our sin.*

Day 12   **Action Plan for Confession
and Restitution**

U

T

E

DAY 7

STRUCTURE:
YOUR DAILY MEDS

*Remember the biblical warning that faith without
deeds is of no value. Without purposeful action,
you're just a passenger, being pulled along without
self-imposed direction or control. Some people prefer
the passenger role. If you are one of those people, you
either need to wake up and take the controls, or
prepare to become one of life's crash test dummies—
and I emphasize DUMMIES.*

—PHILLIP MCGRAW, *LIFE STRATEGIES*

By the time I began seeing a counselor, I'd already repented. I'd thrown out my porn, disconnected my cable service, said good-bye to old friends, relocated to another county, and joined a Bible-believing church—in short, all the "turning from" that needed to be done had been done.

It was a good start, but I couldn't shake this one stubborn question, and by now, I'll bet it's a question that's nagging you too: "I've tried to stop so many times before, only to fail. So why should I think this time will be any different?"

I remembered the countless promises I'd made to God since childhood, promises I'd usually make right after sinning. The bitter tears, the anguished "I swear I'll never do this again!" repeated over and over, then brief weeks (occasionally even months) of abstaining, leading to the belief that *this* time I was finally free.

Then the inevitable longings, temptations, failure, and self-hatred, only to be followed by more futile promises.

So what made me think I'd succeed this time?

It's one of the first questions I posed to my counselor. After hearing about my background, he observed, "You kept failing because you've been making three basic mistakes. First, you've underestimated the power of sexual sin, and you've overestimated your own integrity. You thought just repenting and being sorry would be enough, and that if you really tried, you'd never want to act out again. That's a huge underestimation of sin, not to mention an overestimation of your own strength."

My humility grew a bit that day.

"Second, you failed because you had a change of heart without a change of lifestyle. And without a lifestyle change, all the 'I'm sorrys' in the world won't keep you on track."

I nodded, remembering what John the Baptist had said: "Bear fruits worthy of repentance" (Matthew 3:8). Or, in modern terms, "Show me the money!"

"And finally, it looks like you never set up a routine that would regularly—and I mean daily—influence your heart. The heart is where it all begins, don't you know? Set up daily habits that impact your heart, and you'll set up a structure for success."

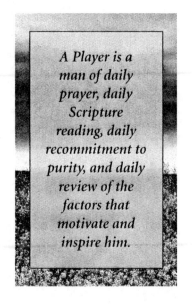

A Player is a man of daily prayer, daily Scripture reading, daily recommitment to purity, and daily review of the factors that motivate and inspire him.

He paused to let it sink in; then he continued: "You've taken the first step. But giving a sin up is never enough. You've got to now set up a structure to keep you from going back to it. In other words, it's time to stop weeping and start working."

THE SUCCESSFUL PLAYER
REPLACES CHAOS WITH STRUCTURE

Where there's sin, there's chaos. That's the nature of sin—it confuses everything and everybody it touches.

It certainly confuses the people who love you. When family members find out the man they've trusted has a secret habit, they often ask, "Well then, who are you? If you're capable of this, what else are you capable of? I'm confused!"

It generates confusion within yourself too. After all, if you publicly say one thing while privately doing another, you're expressing, among other things, confusion. Remember James's description of guys like that: "He is a double-minded man, unstable in all his ways" (James 1:8).

When there's reformation in the church, there's a return to the basics (the authority of the Bible, the need for prayer, the value of worship) and the establishing of order. As a participant in this Game, you're also in a personal reformation. That means you, too, need the order that comes with the basics.

In this part of the process, then, you're going to establish order by incorporating some new habits on a daily, weekly, and monthly basis. That's a lifestyle change; without it, you can't hope to keep playing. The lifestyle change I'm proposing is pretty simple, and I think you'll find that, once you've incorporated it, it doesn't require much beyond simple planning and moderate effort. In other words, this isn't a tough plan to follow, but it's a crucial one.

Here's how it plays out. You're going to develop a structure that includes daily discipline, weekly alliances, and monthly mentoring. All three of these will add some time to your schedule, but not much. And once you've incorporated them, you'll see how easy it is to practice them daily.

Incorporate is a useful term. When you incorporate something, you make it a predictable part of your routine. You've done that with many behaviors—some good, some destructive. Man is, after all, a creature who can incorporate any number of activities until they've evolved into a lifestyle.

So when you began incorporating sexual sin, you repeated it until it became a predictable part of your routine. In doing so, you created what could be called a disease—a combination of secrecy, rebellion, and uncleanness—which has to be avoided in the future. The bad news is that the temptation toward the behavior you've repented of isn't going to vanish. At some point you'll remember the sin you've rejected, and when times get tough, you'll long for it. The good news is that even though the temptation may not vanish, it can certainly be managed by taking your "meds"—your daily, weekly, and monthly structure—which keeps it from overtaking you again.

With that in mind, let's put your structure in place. Today, we'll establish the first part of it through three daily disciplines.

FIRST DISCIPLINE: A DEVOTIONAL LIFE

Let's define *devotional time* as being a time of consistent and focused separation to God. It's a time set apart daily for hearing from Him through the Scripture and communicating with Him in prayer. This is vital to any believer; it's doubly so to you.

Remember, the first and greatest commandment is not to abstain from fornication—serious as that is—rather, it is to love God wholeheartedly and unreservedly. Out of that love comes obedience, the sort Jesus described when He said, "If you love Me, keep My commandments" (John 14:15).

You can't love someone you're not intimate with. Let's make no mistake about this: plenty of men have a relationship with God but not much intimacy with Him. They spend little if any time privately with Him, and while they live a somewhat Christian lifestyle, they lack the vibrant, growing intimacy with Christ that marks a true disciple.

Don't let that be said of you. After all, sexual sin, while hurtful to you and devastating to your loved ones, is first and foremost an offense against God. David acknowledged this in his prayer of repentance after his sin with Bathsheba, when he said, "Against You, You only, have I sinned" (Psalm 51:4).

Since our relationship with God is our primary one, our goal is first and foremost to love Him and to avoid offending Him in the future. But if we're honest, we'll admit that loving Him is, at times, the last thing our rebellious hearts want to do. I'm ashamed to admit it, but I'm not naturally inclined to love Him. I've spent a lifetime loving myself and, at times, even making a god of myself. How, then, can a self-absorbed sinner like me become someone who sincerely loves God?

By knowing Him. To know Him is to love Him, and there's the secret. Apply yourself daily to knowing God through your devotional life, and you will, indeed, grow in your love for Him.

A PLAYER IS A MAN OF THE WORD

Knowing Him means, first, hearing from Him. There are many ways to hear from God: creation speaks of Him, and He communicates through people, events, and a still, small voice within. But all of these can be misinterpreted, and it's unbridled foolishness and risky to rely on any of these as your *primary* way of hearing from God.

The Bible is inspired and infallible, so it's through the Bible that we can be certain we're hearing from God. That means today, and for the rest of your life, you've got to be a man of the Word. Apart from it, you'll never grow closer to Him. And you certainly can't expect to play The Game apart from it. The Psalmist puts it nicely: "Direct my steps by Your word, and let no iniquity have dominion over me" (119:133).

Any serious athlete knows the value of diet. He can't expect his body to perform if it isn't properly fueled, nor can he expect vitamins and supplements (important as they are) to replace food. He eats carefully and well, knowing that he, of all people, can't bypass the value of nutrition.

Likewise, any serious Player knows the value of the Bible because he is, among other things, a man of the Word. He can't expect to stay pure if he's not properly fueled, nor can he expect support groups, seminars, or self-help books (including this one!) to take the place of the Bible. He may use these other resources the way an athlete uses vitamins and supplements, but he never confuses the supplement for the basic diet. He stays in the Word daily, knowing that he, of all people, can't bypass the value of spiritual nutrition.

When you read the Scriptures daily, you get the benefits Paul described to Timothy: "All Scripture is given by inspiration of God, and is profitable for doctrine, for reproof, for correction, for instruction in righteousness, that the man of God may be complete, thoroughly equipped for every good work" (2 Timothy 3:16–17).

You are, then, corrected, built up, instructed, and equipped when you stay daily in the Word. You need all of this and more, so there's simply no excuse for neglecting the Word.

But you may not be in the habit of daily Bible reading. Maybe you've shied away from reading the Bible because you felt it would take too much time or that to really "do it right" you have to read at least five chapters a day. Not so—it's the consistency of Bible reading that matters more than the volume. So if you read one chapter of the Bible daily, that will do you more good than occasionally reading several chapters and then going for days or weeks without reading Scripture at all.

One chapter a day will take you about five minutes. If you're just starting to pick up the Bible, let me suggest you start with the Gospel of John to get a good overview of Christ's life and ministry. Then move on to Romans in the New Testament for a terrific overview of our position in Christ and the responsibilities that come with it; then go back to the Old Testament book of Proverbs for a wonderfully black-and-white, practical blueprint for success. Reading these books one chapter per day will keep you busy for the next sixty-eight days; after that, you can choose for yourself which books of the Bible you'll read. What matters is that you read at least one chapter daily, without exception.

This will add five minutes to your daily routine and is the first leg of your three-part daily structure.

A PLAYER IS A MAN OF PRAYER

By reading the Bible, you hear from God; in prayer, you express yourself to Him. And just as it's impossible to live victoriously apart from the Word, it's inconceivable that you could be a man of purity without also being a man of prayer.

I find it helps to approach prayer *after* reading Scripture, as the Word has a way of roping my thoughts in and bringing me into a more focused frame of mind. I also find it helpful to begin prayer with worship—a simple verbal and mental acknowledgement of who God is. This is in line with the model Christ gave us in Matthew 6:9–13, commonly known as the Lord's Prayer. If you haven't been in the habit of daily prayer, follow this model, using the words He taught us:

"Our Father in heaven, hallowed be Your name" (v. 9). Start by acknowledging who God is, as in: "You're my Father, You're eternal, and You deserve to be worshiped." Name some of the many things He's been to you—your Savior, your Shepherd, your Provider—and name some of His many characteristics (eternal, all-knowing, powerful, gentle, merciful). Starting this way brings you into the right mind-set for serious prayer.

"Your kingdom come. Your will be done, on earth as it is in heaven" (v. 10). Offer your submission. Before asking anything else of Him, ask that His will be worked out in your life.

"Give us this day our daily bread" (v. 11). Make your requests for the day by naming your practical, spiritual, emotional, and physical needs.

"And forgive us our debts, as we forgive our debtors" (v. 12). Confess whatever sins you're aware of. Ask to be cleansed of anything in your thoughts, words, or actions that have hindered your relationship with Him. Then ask for the grace to forgive others, and specifically pray His blessings on the people you forgive.

"And do not lead us into temptation, but deliver us from the evil one" (v. 13). Ask for protection from Satan's attacks, for strength when you're tempted, and for a deeper awareness of the spiritual and eternal implications of everything you do today.

"For Yours is the kingdom and the power and the glory forever.

Amen" (v. 13). End your prayer as you began it—with worship. I
try to end my morning prayers by thanking Him, then declaring
plainly that He is the Lord of my life and asking Him to keep me
aware of that throughout the day.

Build on each of these points, in your own words and your own
way, and you'll develop an effective prayer life. As with your Bible
reading, you shouldn't take on too much here. Just give it a mini-
mum of five minutes daily—remember, consistency not volume is
what counts—and add this to your devotional period.

This, along with reading Scripture, now adds ten minutes to
your daily routine.

Second Discipline:
Recommitment to Sexual Sobriety

This will just take you a few seconds. Say the following sentence
out loud, and think carefully about what you're saying: "Today I
recommit myself to twenty-four hours of sexual sobriety."

To understand the value of this, let's begin by defining *sexual
sobriety*. Being sober, according to the *American College Dictionary*,
means being free from excess, or moderate and temperate. And
while the word *sober* is usually used in contrast to drunkenness, it
applies to other behaviors as well. When applied to sex, it means
sexual conduct that is moderate, controlled, or appropriate.

It's helpful to compare sexual sobriety with sexual purity, because
there's a critical difference. Complete sexual purity is the ideal we
strive toward; sexual sobriety is the standard we require of ourselves.

Complete sexual purity, from a biblical perspective, means absence of any sexually immoral thought, word, or deed. Remember,
Jesus made it clear that sexual sin comes from within: "For from
within, out of the heart of men, proceed evil thoughts, adulteries,
fornications . . . all these evil things come from within and defile a
man" (Mark 7:21–23). James reiterated this in his epistle: "Each
one is tempted when he is drawn away by his own desires and
enticed" (1:14).

And Jesus said even a lusty glance makes you adulterous: "You have heard that it was said to those of old, 'You shall not commit adultery.' But I say to you that whoever looks at a woman to lust for her has already committed adultery with her in his heart" (Matthew 5:27–28).

To achieve complete sexual purity, then, you'd have to reach a point at which you never again have a single immoral thought or look even once at another person—or another person's picture—in the wrong way or for the wrong reason.

Are you up for that? I didn't think so. So if you demand sexual purity of yourself every day, you're bound to fail. Yet you have to keep striving for it, even though you know you'll fall short, because perfection is the ideal we have to strive for daily. We miss the mark yet still reach for it, and every day we get a little closer.

But you can never use that as an excuse for committing overt sexual sins. Just because you won't reach the ideal of complete sexual purity, you can—and must!—meet the standard of sexual sobriety.

Let's illustrate this by looking at what you expect from your pastor. He isn't perfect, right? You expect him to strive toward the ideal of perfection, so that every day he becomes stronger and more Christlike; but he must, at times, fall short. No one is exempt from sin, as the apostle John said: "If we say that we have no sin, we deceive ourselves, and the truth is not in us" (1 John 1:8).

So I'm sure any pastor occasionally loses his temper, has an unkind thought, or fails in some way. When he sins, you expect him to confess and move on, always striving for, though never completely achieving, the ideal of perfection.

Yet there are standards, not just ideals, that you expect him to meet. Your standards for the pastor include that he can't get drunk, he can't fornicate or commit adultery, and he can't steal from the church. These are reasonable standards, and he'll probably need to step down as pastor if he doesn't meet them. If he showed up drunk in the pulpit and your church disciplined him, you'd never excuse his behavior by saying, "Well, nobody's perfect!" After all, nobody's asking him to be *perfect*. But you are requiring him to meet a reasonable *standard*.

So it is with perfect sexual purity versus sexual sobriety. Sadly, you'll always fall short of the first. You'll have some fleeting thoughts, memories, or less-than-pure fantasies for the rest of your life. Take them seriously, confess them in prayer immediately, and with time you'll have them less and less.

But don't ever use that as an excuse for not maintaining sexual sobriety. You may not be sinless, but you can abstain from porn, fornication, adultery, or prostitution. That's what sobriety is about, and that's what you're going to recommit to daily.

Among different organizations, the definition of sexual sobriety varies. The Twelve-Step group Sexaholics Anonymous (SA) defines *sexual sobriety* as refraining from "any form of sex with one's self or with partners other than the spouse." Others—myself included—define *sexual sobriety* as abstaining from the use of pornography or any sex apart from marriage. These are minor but important differences of opinion on the subject; and since sexual sobriety is something you're committing yourself to, you need to decide for yourself which definition to go with.

My definition of *sexual sobriety* is this: "abstaining from pornography or immoral sexual contact with another person." This includes the use of Internet porn or pornographic products of any sort, phone sex, erotic Internet chat rooms, cybersex, strip clubs, prostitutes, erotic massages, premarital sex, or adultery. It all gets down to those ten words: "abstaining from pornography or immoral sexual contact with another person." And believe me, if your definition of sexual sobriety is less than that, you're kidding yourself.

You may be wondering, "What constitutes fornication or adultery? How far can I go with a person before we've sinned?" Let me give you a common-sense guideline: anything you can't do with another person in front of your wife is adultery; anything you can't do with your girlfriend in the middle of church is off-limits. I hope that answers your question!

Sexual sobriety, then, means no porn or immoral contact. That's the standard you're requiring of yourself from now on. If you fall short, you've broken sobriety, meaning you've relapsed and are no longer sexually sober.

THE MASTURBATION QUESTION

We might as well tackle the subject, since we're defining sobriety. Is masturbation a sin? If it is, have you lost your sobriety if you masturbate? Can it be right for some yet wrong for others? As with most tough questions, there is no shortage of contradictory expert opinions. Dr. James Dobson, for example, takes a somewhat lenient view of it in his *Focus on the Family* video series,[7] and Dr. Dwight Carlson condones it outright in his book *From Guilt to Grace*.[8] Author and speaker Dr. Erwin Lutzer of Moody Church in Chicago disagrees, condemning masturbation on moral grounds while conceding that it does no physical harm in *Living with Your Passions*,[9] and the widely respected pastor Jack Hayford refers to it as a rejection of discipleship and personal responsibility.[10]

To muddy things further, I have tremendous respect for all these guys! So who's right? As always, you've got to search the Scriptures yourself and then come to a conclusion. Here's mine:

There are no references to masturbation in the Bible. Some people mistakenly quote the story of Onan, who "spilled his semen on the ground," as a reference to masturbation (Genesis 38:9 NIV). But a closer look at the text shows Onan was in the middle of sexual intercourse, then he withdrew just before ejaculating to avoid impregnating Tamar. He wasn't masturbating; he was practicing a crude form of birth control.

So if there are no clear biblical prohibitions against masturbation, I can't say the Bible specifically condemns it. But I would offer at least three cases which lead me to consider it wrong.

First, since 1 Corinthians 7:4 teaches that a husband's body belongs to his wife, I believe it's wrong for a married man to masturbate. In doing so, he is taking what belongs to his wife and using it only for himself, which seems to be a violation of Paul's guideline in this verse.

Second, Jesus condemned lustful looking and visualizations in Matthew 5:28, and most men visualize a sexual fantasy when they masturbate. So if it's impossible for a man to masturbate without fantasizing, then for him, masturbation is definitely a sin.

Finally, Paul said that anything a man does without faith—that is, anything a man does that he feels badly about, even if it's not forbidden in Scripture—is, for him, a sin (Romans 14:23). So even if a man is single and has the ability to masturbate without fantasizing, if he feels it's wrong to masturbate, then for him, it's wrong.

For these reasons, I'm convinced masturbation is usually, if not always, inherently wrong. But if you're a man who's single, can masturbate without fantasizing, and your conscience is clear when you do it, then I cannot with integrity say you're sinning. That's a matter you'll have to consider in prayer and (I hope) with some guidance from your pastor as well.

Make two decisions, then. First, decide whether or not masturbation is, under your circumstances, sinful. Second, if you've determined it's a sin, decide whether or not it constitutes breaking your sobriety if you do it.

One last thought on this tough subject: if you decide that masturbating means you've broken sobriety, that's fine. But know that abstaining from masturbation, especially if you're single, is extremely difficult and probably will take repeated attempts and failures. (Ask anyone who's tried, if you can find someone who'll really talk about it!) So be patient with yourself, and especially be in prayer for grace as you learn to abstain from this behavior. (For a discussion on abstaining from masturbation, see "Masturbation" in the appendix.)

THE SOBRIETY INVESTMENT

Once you've defined sobriety, start counting the number of days you've stayed sober. This is a helpful way of measuring your progress and keeping up your motivation. After all, the longer you've stayed sober, the more reluctant you'll be to break your winning streak. So keep track of your length of sobriety, and once you've established an accountability group and partner, keep them updated on your sobriety as well. They'll be celebrating each week, month, and year you accrue, and those celebrations will be indescribably meaningful to you.

Every day, then, you'll recommit yourself verbally to sexual sobriety by saying (out loud, preferably), "For the next twenty-four hours, I recommit myself to sexual sobriety."

This sets a course for the rest of the day. It's not a "magic saying," but it's a way of setting your thoughts and efforts in the right direction. It takes only a few seconds, but it will, if used daily, influence the many decisions you make either to resist or yield to sexual temptation. When you've begun the day with this recommitment, you're far more likely to catch yourself when you consider lusting, sexually fantasizing, or acting out.

So begin this today as part of your disciplines. I've used it for years and have been pleased with the impact it has had on my thought life and general integrity.

Third Discipline: Motive Review

Knowing right from wrong is seldom the problem. Staying motivated to do what we know is right (and to *not* do what we know is wrong)—now *there's* the challenge.

To meet it, you're going to incorporate one more daily discipline we'll call motive review. By including this with your daily devotionals, you'll be starting each day with a reminder of the reasons you want to stay on track. That helps keep your motivation to say no to sexual temptation alive and fresh.

Motivation changes. Some days you're strongly inspired to do what's right. But other days, for reasons not always obvious, you may feel as though you couldn't care less. And since those days can't be predicted—that is, you can't foretell how "pumped" you're going to be on a given day—you need to incorporate a habit that routinely gives you a fresh shot of motivation.

Your motive review will do that. I find it's similar to my first cup of coffee in the morning. I don't expect to pop out of bed alert and energized, because I'm anything but that when I get up! But I can require a simple task of myself: I can put one foot in front of the other, stumble over to the coffeepot, turn it on, wait for the magic brew to drip down, and then drink it. In other words, I can't wake up wired and ready to go. But I *can* expose myself to the beverage that will get me there.

So it is with motivation. You may not wake up inspired to do what's right. But you can expose yourself to your motive review list—your list of reasons for staying clean—and that list becomes your mental cup of coffee, thereby getting yourself energized to take on the day.

Developing the list is simple. On your computer or on a sheet of paper, list thirty-five lines. Each line needs to be filled in with the reasons you're motivated to stay pure. You'll notice I've started you off with five reasons that, I'm sure, apply to anyone. Now you fill in the rest. Think of the things that matter the most to you—the people you love, the life you want, the physical and emotional health you're aiming for—and write down thirty of them until the list is filled.

Then, after your daily devotions and recommitment, read this list aloud. It will be a mental reminder to you of the reasons you had a crisis of truth, and it will emotionally jump-start you by reminding you of what matters the most. That, in turn, will pump up your motivation, keeping it alive and intact.

This motive review—along with your Scripture reading, prayer, and recommitment—will add a total of fifteen minutes to your daily routine. You and I both know you can spare fifteen extra minutes a day to make a much-needed lifestyle change. There's a good chance, in fact, you've invested more time than that incorporating behaviors that have nearly destroyed your life! So surely you can find the time to incorporate new habits that will keep you on track.

No excuses, please. This daily structure—a simple fifteen-minutes-a-day plan that's easy to follow and nondemanding—makes up what we call your daily meds. Develop them now; take them daily. Because no one can win The Game without them.

DAY 8

ACTION PLAN FOR STRUCTURE

KEY VERSE

Take heed to yourself and to the doctrine. Continue in them, for in doing this you will save both yourself and those who hear you.

—1 TIMOTHY 4:16

PRINCIPLE

When we repent of sexual sin, we frequently leave a huge void in our lives that has, up to this point, been filled with wrong behaviors. To keep ourselves from returning to them, we need to incorporate new behaviors that will provide checks and balances.

ACTION

1. Plan your daily discipline period by blocking out a fifteen-minute time slot and reserving that slot daily. Write down the time:

   Daily discipline period: from _____ to _____ (a.m. / p.m.)

2. Choose and write down the book of the Bible you're going to begin reading daily. _____.

3. Incorporate at least five minutes for prayer to follow your Bible reading. Make sure this time includes worship, confession, and petitions.

4. Decide whether or not your definition of sexual sobriety will include abstinence from masturbation. Then begin making a daily verbal recommitment by saying the following out loud: "Today, I recommit myself to another twenty-four hours of sexual sobriety."

5. List (or type into your computer) thirty reasons you are personally motivated to stay away from the behavior you've rejected. After completing this list, be sure to read it once daily after your devotions.

RATIONALE

The checks and balances of our daily disciplines serve a threefold purpose:

1. They solidify our intimacy with God, which is crucial for recovery.
2. They enhance our hatred of sin and love of righteousness.
3. They keep us on course when we're tempted or discouraged, thus serving as "meds" to help keep our condition at bay.

PRAYER

Father, when I repented, I meant it with all my heart. But even now, I confess I'm inclined to wander. I have the conflicting desires of a servant and a rebel, a son and a renegade. So help me, as I develop these structures in my life, to stay consistent when I'm inclined to be unreliable, to stay focused when I'm drawn to laziness, and to allow Your Word and the bonds You and I develop in prayer to sink so deeply in my heart that I am, indeed, shepherded by You and want nothing more than to stay under Your yoke. I ask this in Jesus's name. Amen.

DAY 9

ALIGNMENT:
TEAMMATES AND ALLIES

She flashed a brilliant smile . . . he knew this
would be his last chance to run. But he was
dizzy and weak. Running would require more
strength than he could possibly muster.
"Come on, Mitch."
He surveyed the beach and, of course, saw no one.
"I can't do this," he muttered through clenched teeth.
"But I want you."
"I can't do it."
"Come on, Mitch. No one will ever know."
No one will ever know. No one will ever know.
He walked slowly toward her.
No one will ever know . . .

—JOHN GRISHAM, *THE FIRM*

For the first twenty-nine years of my life I believed my sin was, and
would always remain, my little secret.

And I was determined to keep it that way.

After all, I reasoned, could anyone—especially anyone in the
church—understand what it's like to wrestle with sexual lust?
Could anyone be trusted with my secrets? And what good would
telling do, anyway? I already knew right from wrong, so the last
thing I needed was to confide in someone about my struggles, only

to have him whip out a few Bible verses on sexual sin (verses I already knew by heart, thank you!) and insult me with some "just say no" advice. Those weren't the kind of answers I needed.

So I kept my sexual sin hidden, and I was ashamed, isolated, and (I thought) incurably defective. It's easy to believe you're a freak—or at least a second-class, second-rate Christian—when you don't let anyone know you well enough to prove that you're wrong. And it's doubly easy to believe the sin you're hiding will always stay hidden when you've spent a lifetime covering it up. So each time you indulge, you repeat the same lie over and over: "No one will ever know, no one will ever know . . ."

Your next step, then, is to make sure someone *does* know.

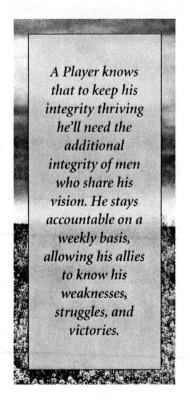

A Player knows that to keep his integrity thriving he'll need the additional integrity of men who share his vision. He stays accountable on a weekly basis, allowing his allies to know his weaknesses, struggles, and victories.

WHERE THERE'S GODLY WORK, THERE'S GODLY ALLIANCE

Nehemiah had a "crisis of truth" when he heard Jerusalem's walls were crumbled and her streets overrun with rubbish. After weeping and repenting, he pursued a vision to rebuild her by enlisting allies (Nehemiah 2:17–18). Solomon did the same in constructing the temple, when he found the best engineers to design and erect it (1 Kings 5–6). And Saul of Tarsus, when he was blinded and humbled en route to Damascus, needed allies to lead him by the hand and then baptize, comfort, and instruct him on his way toward becoming the apostle Paul (Acts 9:10–19). These men learned what every Player knows: you cannot and will not play The Game without allies.

Your allies are the men you connect with who share your vision to rebuild. They share your desire to be healthy and holy, they believe in your potential and theirs as well, and they're aligned with you as together you grow stronger each week.

They are, in other words, your teammates. And don't think for a minute you can win without them, because they provide something critical and irreplaceable: additional integrity.

I think you already have some integrity, and I have some too. But that's the problem—we have *some*, and *some* isn't enough! When temptations hit hard, I need *lots* of integrity to resist them. But my own history proves my integrity levels aren't always high enough. So I need the additional integrity of my accountability partner and group, because when mine runs low, I have theirs to fill in the gap. And their integrity, combined with my own, *is* enough!

Watch a couple of workout partners in the gym, and you'll see this principle in action. When two guys decide to work out together, they share a mutual vision. Both of them want to get stronger, leaner, and healthier. Both are ready to sacrifice time and effort to achieve their goal, but both know that at times their motivation—or integrity, if you will—may be low. During those "off days" (which we all have), they'll be tempted to renege on their commitment by not putting much effort into their workout or by staying home from the gym altogether.

So they make a covenant, based on their desire to be physically fit and their awareness that, at times, their motivation will be low. They agree to meet at the gym at a certain time, where they'll push each other hard. So while they're pumping iron, if one feels weak or unmotivated, the other will get in his face, sometimes even screaming, "*Push* it! One more rep! *Harder!*"

That's the value of your allies, the men to whom you choose to be accountable. They meet with you weekly, because they share your vision to get pure and stay pure. They also know that at times their motivation, and yours, may be low, and that during those "off days" (which—admit it!—we all have), you or they will be tempted to renege on your commitment by yielding to sexual temptation.

So you make a covenant with them, based on your motivation to be sexually sober and your awareness that, at times, your motivation may be down. You agree to meet weekly to question each other and to hold each other accountable. And if one of you stumbles or feels weak and unmotivated, the other one exhorts him by getting in his face: "*Push* it! I *know* you can make it! *Harder!*"

The author of Hebrews had something to say about this: "Exhort one another daily, while it is called 'Today,' lest any of you be hardened through the deceitfulness of sin" (3:13). Our tendency, left on our own, is to kid ourselves, compromise, and develop a general hardheartedness toward sin. Good preventive care, then, includes the benefit of mutual exhortation.

To *exhort* means literally to come alongside, beseech, cheer up, and implore someone. It's derived from the same word Jesus used when He promised the Holy Spirit would be our "Comforter"— One who would come alongside, beseech, cheer up, and implore. So your allies are not only aligned with you, but they're aligned with the Holy Spirit as well; and they are the people whom He uses to do His work in you.

THE ACCOUNTABILITY STRUCTURE

Your allies at this point need to be made up of one accountability partner you'll meet with once a week and an accountability group you'll meet with weekly as well. Keep both these alliances in place for the next six months. Then if you've consistently stayed clean from the sin you rejected in Section One (Repentance), you can stop meeting with either your group or your partner—but stop only one, not both. You'll need to incorporate ongoing accountability as a permanent habit, so at the end of six months, you can decide whether you'll get it through a group or a partner. Let's look at how each works and what the advantages of each are.

THE ACCOUNTABILITY PARTNERSHIP

When you form an accountability partnership, you commit to meeting with one man weekly, usually for thirty minutes, to ask each other specific questions about your areas of weakness. So, for example, if you repented of pornography in Section One, your partner will ask you once a week whether you've continued to stay clean from porn and whether you've done anything to compromise your purity. You'll ask him similar questions about his area of weakness, whatever that may be.

Your questions need to be specific, and each of you needs to provide the other with the right questions to ask. So again, suppose you've been viewing pornography on the Internet. Suppose you're also a married man whose wife recently found out about the porn, and you're trying to restore her trust. In that case, you'd write down a few questions for your partner to ask you, and they'd look something like this:

1. Did you look at pornography this week?

2. Did you masturbate this week?

3. Did you keep up with your disciplines this week?

4. Did you and your wife pray together this week?

5. Did you let yourself look inappropriately at other women this week?

6. Have you answered these questions honestly?

You'd then give these to your partner, and he'd give you the questions to ask him as well. You'd then agree to ask each other these questions weekly and to answer them honestly.

There's good reason for being specific about these questions and for writing them out in advance. If you did relapse and use porn during the week, there's a good chance you won't want to admit it. (Remember, our first tendency when we sin is to cover it up and avoid dealing with it.) So you'll be prone to avoid the subject altogether unless you're asked specifically about it. That's why accountability partners should never sit down at their weekly meeting and say:

"So, how was your week?"

"Fine. How about yours?"

"Fine."

"Good. Nice talking to you."

That doesn't accomplish much, and it allows a man to avoid coming clean. So make your questions specific, and make sure they fully cover your areas of weakness.

If by chance you or your partner has to answer yes to any of these questions, the other partner is *not* there to condemn or punish him. Rather, he's there to exhort—that is, to build up, encourage, and come alongside.

So if you had answered yes when your partner asked if you'd used porn, his job would be to encourage you to not give up. He'd also ask if there was anything you could do differently in the future to prevent repeating the same mistake and if there's anything he can do at this point to help. The conversation might go something like this:

"Did you use porn this week?"

"Hate to admit it, but yeah, I backslid and looked at some porn on the Internet. And I hate myself for it!"

"Wow, sorry to hear it. OK, let's try to keep this from happening again. First of all, do you have a filter on your Internet?"

"Nope, I still haven't gotten one."

"OK, will you promise me you'll get one installed this week? Because I really think you'll wind up using the porn again if you don't get some on-line protection."

"Will do. By next week, I'll have that in place, so be sure to hold me to this when we meet."

"OK, I will. And how's this affected you spiritually?"

"Pretty badly. I feel like an absolute loser."

"Which is exactly what Satan wants you to think. Try not to wallow in this, OK? I'm really glad you're sorry over your sin, but beating yourself up won't help anything. Let's make this week a new start and do it better this time around, OK? You're in my prayers. I know you can make it."

Notice the partner's tone? Supportive, practical, specific. That's good accountability in practice, and it works. And believe me, this can (and probably will) become one of your most valued relationships.

Finding an accountability partner will take some time and legwork. The kind of guy you're looking for as a partner should have the following qualifications:

1. He should be a committed Christian.

2. He should be working on his own purity and realize the value of accountability as he does so.

3. He should be mature enough to make and keep a weekly thirty-minute commitment.

4. He should be willing to ask and answer specific accountability questions like the ones mentioned earlier.

5. He should be able to keep personal information to himself, without sharing it with his wife or other people.

You can locate that sort of man either through your current circle of friends, or your church fellowship, Sunday school class, or men's ministry group. You might also look into existing men's groups like Promise Keepers or Celebrate Recovery.

In tomorrow's action plan, we'll cover some of the ways to locate these groups, find a potential accountability partner, and get the weekly meetings established. For now, I just want to make sure you've grasped the importance of the accountability partnership and the principles it involves.

THE ACCOUNTABILITY GROUP

As valuable as an accountability partner is, there are benefits a group brings that one-on-one accountability can't. An accountability group provides built-in community with men who understand your weaknesses and who celebrate your victories. It also provides what I call "group wisdom," which is the benefit of other men's accumulated wisdom and experience. That's especially valuable because we all have our blind spots—those areas of behavior or attitude we're unaware of, but that really do need some work! There's nothing like the alliance of a good accountability group to help us see, and correct, those blind spots.

An accountability group is more than a Bible study or prayer group. Those are great, of course, but they usually don't provide accountability. You can attend them without ever letting the other group members know how you're really doing, because these types of groups are not set up for self-disclosure. For a group to qualify as an accountability group, it has to have two elements:

1. The group members should know about the specific sexual sin you've struggled with.

2. The group members should know, on a weekly basis, how successful you've been in resisting that sin and how your spiritual and emotional progress has been as well.

You can locate a group by asking your pastor if he has any recommendations or by locating any men's ministries in your area that provide accountability. You can also check the following Web sites:

- Celebrate Recovery (www.celebraterecovery.com)
  Celebrate Recovery is an Eight-Step Christian group
  originating from Rick Warren's Saddleback Valley
  Community Church in Southern California with branches
  in churches across the country.

- Promise Keepers (www.promisekeepers.org)
  PK groups are inspired by the Promise Keepers men's
  movement and are excellent resources for Christ-centered
  accountability.

- Overcomer's Outreach (www.overcomersoutreach.org)
  Overcomer's Outreach is a Christian-based program

addressing many life-dominating behaviors, including sexual sin.

All of these are Christian-based groups, and their Web sites will direct you to the group meetings nearest to you. Tomorrow, your action plan will include locating one of these groups and attending it next week. That, combined with your weekly meetings with your partner, will provide the additional integrity you'll need to stay in The Game.

Remember, being a Player means accepting a hard, unchanging fact: you're not in this alone. You're a member of the body of Christ; and when you suffer, we all suffer. Likewise, when you get stronger, we all benefit. Good accountability reminds you of that and so much more.

I know, because when I'm tempted, my ability to resist is strengthened—*hugely* strengthened, really—when I remember that each week I will be telling my partner whether or not I yielded to temptation. When I allowed myself to indulge in whatever sin I fancied, I was operating under the myth of independence. I not only assumed no one would ever know—I also assumed it was nobody's business, so why *should* they know? Then I learned the hard way how stupid those assumptions were.

I trust you'll be smarter than I was. You're not your own; your decisions bring consequences. They will, at some point, bear either good or bitter fruit, so settle it now, once and for all. "No one will know" is a myth. Someone will know; someone does know. So let's set up a structure that will help you to never forget it.

DAY 10

ACTION PLAN FOR ALIGNMENT

KEY VERSE

But exhort one another daily, while it is called "Today," lest any of you be hardened through the deceitfulness of sin.

—HEBREWS 3:13

PRINCIPLE

Left on our own, no matter how sincere our commitment to purity, we'll be inclined to compromise when the going gets tough. That's because our own integrity isn't always sufficient to sustain us. For that reason, we of all people need the benefit of regular and rigorous accountability.

ACTION

1. Locate an accountability group in your area. Begin with your church and see if there are any men's accountability groups available. If not, ask your pastor or a leader in your church if there are any groups in the area he would recommend. If he doesn't know of any, check the Internet for the following group Web sites:

Celebrate Recovery (www.celebraterecovery.com)

Promise Keepers (www.promisekeepers.org)

Overcomer's Outreach (www.overcomersoutreach.org)

2. Determine the day and time of the next group meeting, and be certain to attend. Jot down, after the group, what benefits you got from it and what questions or concerns you need to bring up at the next group meeting.

   Note: If, after you've checked with your pastor and have checked the Internet and any other available resources, you're still unable to locate a group in your area, then consider beginning one yourself. This is only to be done as a last resort! But if it's your only recourse, take the following steps:

   a. Consult with your pastor, and get his blessing and permission to begin facilitating a group. Ask if he or any staff member would be willing to lead it; if not, then you may need to facilitate it yourself.

   b. With your pastor, determine where and when your meetings will take place and how to let your church know about the formation of your group.

   c. In your group meetings, use a book, such as this one. That will give you a format and good educational material.

   d. Stay in close communication with someone who has experience in this area as you begin your group. You'll need guidance and encouragement, so be sure to stay connected.

3. Begin looking for an accountability partner. Think of someone who might be available either from your circle of Christian friends or your Sunday school class, church fellowship, or men's group. Remember the qualities you're looking for:

   a. He should be a committed Christian.

   b. He should be working on his own purity and realize the value of accountability as he does so.

c. He should be mature enough to make and keep a weekly thirty-minute commitment.

d. He should be willing to ask and answer specific accountability questions such as the ones mentioned above.

e. He should be able to keep personal information to himself, without sharing it with his wife or other people.

There's a good chance you're not going to find someone today. Give yourself two weeks for this, because you'll have to look around, make some calls, and ask some questions. Here's a good way to present yourself to someone you'd like to partner with: "I've had some struggles with sexual sin, and I'm working hard on trying to stay away from it. So I'm working this plan that includes accountability." Then show him Day 9 of this book, and ask him if this looks like something he'd like to try with you.

4. Develop the questions your partner will need to ask you. Jot down at least five specific questions based on your areas of weakness and vision. Be specific!

RATIONALE

Accountability alliances have to be built through careful planning, legwork, and strategy. You need to begin by planning your structure. Then pursue it by inquiring ("What groups/which people are available?"), choosing ("Which group will I join/whom will I ask to be a partner?"), and acting on your choices.

PRAYER

Lord, letting someone in on my struggles seems like one of the hardest things You've asked me to do. This is new territory for me, and my shame and self-consciousness get in the way and cause me any number of fears. Give me the courage, then, to make myself known, both the good and the bad. Give me the faith I need to believe You can provide me with allies who will share my vision without judging or belittling me, and remove from me the habits of secrecy and isolation that have kept me in bondage for so many years. I ask this in Jesus's name. Amen.

DAY 11

CONFESSION AND RESTITUTION

If someone you love is living a lie, it makes you feel crazy inside. You have this inner sense that something is wrong but you don't know what it is. And every time you try to find out what's going on, you either get accused of something that you're not guilty of or you get lied to again. So you're lonely. So lonely! You're trying to engage, you're trying to share your heart, and it's like you hit a wall every time.

—LAURIE HALL, *AN AFFAIR OF THE MIND*

I sat across the restaurant table from Elaine, as nervous and fidgety as a fifteen-year-old on his first date. But I was no teenager. It was the spring of 1984, I was twenty-nine, and my jumpiness must have seemed odd to her.

We had a history together, after all. Six years earlier, we'd had a brief affair. She became pregnant and aborted our child, then I broke things off abruptly with her and plunged into sexual perversion. She'd tried communicating with me over the years, and I'd rebuffed her. Worse yet, before our affair, I'd been a staff pastor at her church, where she'd sat under my preaching and teaching. So my nervousness that night sprang from shame. I'd let her down horribly and had no idea how to express my sorrow.

"I asked you here so I could apologize to you," I finally said after we ordered. "But anything I say is going to sound so stupid."

Elaine shot me a curious, cynical look. For six years I'd

ignored her, never returning her calls, treating her like a discarded toy. Her eyes said it all: *Since when do you ever feel sorry about anything?*

I deserved that look. I sputtered, ransacked my vocabulary for the right words and came up empty, then finally blurted, "I've repented. Three months ago. I'm back in church."

That got a response!

"Well, not preaching, of course. But I'm back with the Lord. And I'm trying to contact the people I let down so I can apologize, and I can't think of anyone I let down more than I did you."

She shook her head and smiled, saying nothing, and I felt like the very definition of a fool. I had waves of "I'm sorrys" wanting to burst out of me, but how would "I'm sorry" undo the hurt I'd caused her?

I was about to give up and leave when she put out her hand, grabbed mine, and said, "At least tell me that you know how badly you hurt me. Then tell me how you're going to avoid hurting people from now on."

SURVEYING THE DAMAGE

When Nehemiah set out to rebuild Jerusalem, he began by taking a close look at the damage done to the city walls (Nehemiah 2:11–16). It couldn't have been easy. Knowing the walls were decayed was one thing; closely inspecting them to see just *how* decayed was another. But how else could he rebuild? To make things right, he had to first see how *wrong* they really were.

When you sinned sexually, someone else was probably damaged as well. Certainly your partner in the sin (if there was a partner) was hurt, and you did damage to yourself. Those closest to you, though, were also affected, sometimes in ways too horrible to consider. But you can't move on until you *have* considered them, assessing them just like Nehemiah assessed the walls: up close and personal. That's how rebuilding begins.

Jesus placed such importance on this that He commanded we

drop everything—even our acts of worship!—if we have un-
finished business with someone we've wronged: "Therefore if
you bring your gift to the altar, and there remember that your
brother has something against you, leave your gift there before
the altar, and go your way. First
be reconciled to your brother,
and then come and offer your
gift" (Matthew 5:23–24).

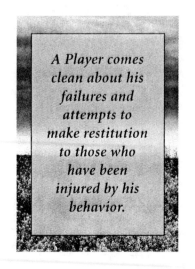

> *A Player comes clean about his failures and attempts to make restitution to those who have been injured by his behavior.*

It's not enough to confess your
sin. You're also required to do
whatever is possible to relieve the
effect your sin had on others.

This especially applies if you're
married, because you've betrayed
your wife at such a primary level.
If you're single, it's also possible
you've disappointed friends or
family members or (as in my
case) people in the church who've
depended on you. At any rate, you now have a twofold responsibility: restitution and rebuilding. And while this chapter applies
mostly to married readers, I hope you'll read it carefully even if
you're single, because you'll gain some insight into the havoc
that sexual sin wreaks on a marriage. (You can also use these
principles to repair any damaged relationship you may be dealing with.)

A PLAYER OWNS HIS ERRORS

To make restitution, you need to restore what you took from
another person or, in some cases, what you caused another person
to lose. So if your wife discovered your sin, you've caused her to
lose something. She's lost a few "somethings," in fact, and looking
at these losses is a painful but necessary part of your process. So
walk with me as we examine them, one by one, at close range.

ASSUMPTIONS

Your wife has lost her *assumptions.* All close relationships are based on assumptions, you know. We assume we pretty well know the person we're relating to; we assume their word is good; we assume our trust in them is well placed. And if that's true of close relationships in general, it's especially true of marriage.

Your wife assumed the two of you were monogamous. And why not? Isn't that exactly what you promised her at the altar—to forsake all others and cleave only to her? She also assumed your word was good, that your vows were sacred and unbreakable, and that she would never have to question the integrity of the man she was joining herself to.

For that matter, she probably assumed she knew all your "deep, dark secrets." She knew you weren't perfect, but she figured she knew whatever quirks you had—some were endearing, some were exasperating, but none, she thought, were really serious—so there'd be no big surprises in store for her.

In other words, she assumed she was safe with you.

Then the rug got pulled out from under her, and she made the horrible discovery that she was wrong about so many things. Wrong about her marriage, wrong about you, wrong about the assumptions she'd taken for granted. And when they came crashing down and shattering all around her, she began wondering, *Was I right about anything? Was everything I believed a myth? Did I ever really know this man?*

Your wife is in mourning. She's suffered the death of her assumptions.

ATTRACTIVENESS

She also may have lost confidence in her *attractiveness.* As you read this, there are women around the world looking into their mirrors, hating what they're seeing. They didn't always hate their image— they may not have thought of themselves as gorgeous, but they felt they had at least some beauty or charm to offer their husbands, and they rejoiced in that.

Until the day they discovered their husbands preferred other women to them. Or other men. Or pornographic images. Or whatever. And that discovery has blown away their physical confidence.

"I used to think I was OK to look at," a wife in that position often says. "But I've seen the pictures he's been looking at, and that's obviously what he prefers over me. And I can't compete!" She looks at the surgically enhanced bodies of the porn stars her husband has been lusting after, then she looks at her own body, and suddenly she's ashamed of herself.

She doesn't realize her husband's sin probably has nothing to do with her looks. Married men by the score cheat on beautiful wives, which certainly isn't a reflection on the wives. The love of the chase, the flattery of an affair, the convenience of a hooker or a stripper— these are just some of the features attracting married men to adulterous behavior. But their wives seldom know that, so they often assume they're to blame. *If only I were more this or less that*, they think, and their sadness over not being "more this or less that" can be overwhelming.

In many cases, they've lost the joy they took in their femininity, leaving them feeling ugly, unacceptable, and unwanted.

INTELLIGENCE

She has also lost confidence in her *intelligence*. "Stupid me!" a wife exclaims when her husband's secret behavior is finally exposed. "He said he was working late, and I believed him!" Or, "He said he didn't know how those porn sites showed up on our computer history, so I took his word." Or, "Every time I asked, 'Are you having an affair?' he kept denying it and saying I was paranoid, and I swallowed his lies! I must be an idiot!"

She's wrong, of course, because she doesn't realize her husband has probably been committing this sin for so long—and lying about it while covering it up—that he's become a pro at deception. And if you've been fooled by a professional liar, that doesn't mean you're stupid. It just means he's good.

But she doesn't realize that, so she begins wondering just how stupid she really is. In a case like that, the husband hasn't just made the wife feel *pain*. He's also made her feel *brainless*.

CONFIDENCE IN GOD

She may have even lost *confidence in God*. We know that everything we experience has been allowed by Him. So when our experiences are painful, we're prone to wonder *why* He allowed them. And few things can make a woman question God's purposes like a husband's sexual sin.

One of the saddest remarks I've ever heard in my office came from a wife who found out her husband was in an adulterous relationship. "If my daddy knew that the man who wanted to marry me would hurt me someday," she said through her tears, "he'd have shot that guy before he'd let him marry me! But my heavenly Father, who knows everything, allowed me to marry a man who wound up shattering my heart! Why would God give me to this man, when He knew this man would crush me? I guess I don't even matter to God anymore."

Please take a moment to read that last sentence again. Twice.

When you broke your wife's heart, there's a good chance she remembered that God gave her to you. And she wondered, as any child would, why her Daddy handed her over to someone so hurtful.

MAKING RESTITUTION:
ACKNOWLEDGE, EXPRESS, AND CLARIFY

You may be tempted, in light of all this, to give up. I've been the bad guy before, so I know the helplessness that comes with facing your sin. It can't be undone, and you can't give your wife (or anyone else you've hurt) a pill to relieve the pain you caused. That can leave a man feeling like there's no point in even trying to make it right, because what can he do about the unalterable past and the heartache it's created?

"If only . . ."

Miserable words, aren't they? I've heard hundreds of sorrowing husbands mutter them in my office. "If only I'd been thinking right, if only I'd stopped before I got caught, if only . . ."

But there's a better way. You can't erase the sordid facts—you sinned, your wife's in pain, and your marriage is damaged. But damaged marriages can be rebuilt, and you can begin the rebuilding now with three simple actions.

ACKNOWLEDGE

Acknowledge what you have done. An acknowledgement is a statement of recognition. To begin rebuilding your marriage, make an acknowledgement—or a confession, if you prefer to call it that—in three parts.

First, tell her you acknowledge the nature of your sin. It's not enough to say, "I committed adultery" or, "I used pornography." That's only a partial confession, because it acknowledges the action, but not the nature of the action.

Acknowledging the nature of the sin means you've looked at both the sin and its implications. It means you realize you've not only sinned against your wife. You've also betrayed her, and a loved one's betrayal is one of the worst of all human experiences.

You also acknowledge that you've insulted her by replacing her, however briefly, with something cheap, counterfeit, and tawdry. You've neglected her, too, as you jumped right over her needs to satisfy your lust. She needed your sexual energy, your attention, your affection, your time, and your heart, all of which you gave to someone else (or several "someone elses"), thereby ignoring the one person who truly deserved them.

She needs to hear that you understand all of this. Tell her.

Second, tell her you acknowledge the consequences of your behavior. Make sure she knows you're aware of the impact your sin has had. That will answer the question I've heard from too many wives: "Does he have a clue as to how much pain he's caused?"

Don't let yours be one of the wives who wonder about that. Make sure she knows that you know both what you've done and the effect it's had on her. Acknowledge to her that you've shattered her trust and that she may be unable to believe anything you say for some time. Acknowledge how difficult it must be for her to be civil to you and how crushing it must be to wonder if she'll ever feel safe with you again. Acknowledge the fact that you've struck a blow to your home and marriage, and you know it's a blow that came down hard.

You already know that. Now let her know that you know.

Third, acknowledge your limited ability to understand the pain you've caused. Tell her that you can't fully understand the hurt because (and this is vital) you did it to her; she didn't do it to you.

Sometimes it's insulting to tell someone you know exactly how he or she feels, because there's a good chance you don't. In this case, there's more than a good chance. You've done something to your wife that she probably hasn't done to you, so how can you really understand what she's going through?

Acknowledge the fact that you can't fully appreciate her pain, because it's just that: *her* pain, courtesy of her husband. Admit that you can't fully relate to it, but then give her this gift: ask her to explain her pain to you.

Tell her that you want to know what she's going through and that you'd like to understand it better. Promise that you'll simply listen, without interrupting or defending yourself, as she tells you what it was like learning about your sin—the shock, the fear, the disbelief—and what it's like dealing with the aftermath of it. Listen carefully while she tells you this, and make sure she knows you're listening.

Then never, never forget what you heard. And see that you'll never have to hear it again.

But acknowledgement isn't enough, is it? You can acknowledge a wrongdoing without ever showing you feel anything about it. You know what you've done, but does it matter to you?

I think it does. You *know* it does. But does she?

EXPRESS

The next step is to express your pain to her. Tell her you're hurting, too, and that just as you can't fully understand her pain, nor can she fully understand yours, because yours is the pain of the villain.

You live with daily shame, hourly regret. It haunts you, intruding on your thoughts during your workday and keeping you awake at night. And it will go on hurting for a long, long time.

So express your pain. Let her know you'll die wishing this never happened, and even though you'll always be grateful for her forgiveness, forgiving yourself will be a lifelong challenge. She may someday let it go, but you? Never. Let her know this will never, never be OK with you.

Express yourself to her, and don't hold back. Your lady needs to see that her man not only recognizes his sin but also feels something about it—and about her.

CLARIFY

But don't stop there. Acknowledge your sin and express your pain, but then clarify your intention and recovery plan. Because, after all, what good are tears if they're not followed by action?

Your intention is to stay sober and do what's necessary to restore your marriage. That's simple enough: clarify it. But remember, you have a credibility problem. So give her more than an intention. Clarify your recovery plan as well. In other words, don't just tell her you intend to stay sober. Tell her *how*. And the best way to tell her is to show her.

Show her a copy of your action plans from Days 8 and 10. Tell her this is the plan you're following to stay on track. Then tell her that, although you don't necessarily expect her to believe you, you do hope she'll watch you.

Then stick to the plan. Observe your disciplines daily, no exceptions. Develop and use your accountability structure. Follow The Game Plan to the letter, making sure she knows what it is, so she'll know what to look for. That sets the stage for rebuilding trust.

Trust is only rebuilt through a combination of time and consistency. She can decide to forgive you, certainly, but no one can decide to trust. If someone has betrayed you, you stop trusting that person. And once that happens, you can't turn the trust back on. It can only grow when the person who broke your trust shows consistency over a period of time.

So you, as a husband who has shattered his wife's trust, have your work cut out for you. Patiently and consistently follow your program with a servant's heart and an eye toward restoring peace in your home; and in due time, you'll reap the rewards.

If you're truly repentant, then, you'll do these three things:

1. You'll confess your sin without minimizing it.

2. You'll express sincere remorse over your failures.

3. You'll develop (and stick to) a verifiable recovery plan.

Then you'll wait for trust and intimacy to bloom again in your home. And you'll know that although you cannot undo, you certainly can, by God's grace, rebuild.

DAY 12

ACTION PLAN FOR CONFESSION AND RESTITUTION

KEY VERSE

So husbands ought to love their own wives as their own bodies; he who loves his wife loves himself. For no one ever hated his own flesh, but nourishes and cherishes it, just as the Lord does the church.

—EPHESIANS 5:28–29

PRINCIPLE

When the one we love is injured by our sexual sin, it's as though we've struck a blow to ourselves. As a man called to love his wife as Christ loved the church, you have a calling to sacrificially care for her while she's in the throes of pain over betrayal and confusion, and you can care for her through restitution and rebuilding. (Note: If you're unmarried, consider whether there's someone whom you need to make restitution to, and if so, apply these steps to your relationship with that person. If not, you can skip the steps in today's action plan.)

ACTION

1. Sit down with your wife and acknowledge your behavior, its consequences, and your inability to fully understand her pain. Use this time to express your remorse as well and to help her understand the steps you're now taking (through your daily disciplines and weekly accountability) to stay sexually sober.

Sample message to your wife (use your own words, but as a guideline, this may help): "I know what I've done, and I've done more than commit a sexual sin. I've betrayed you by breaking a sacred promise I made before you and God. That betrayal must have shattered you, and you've got every reason to be enraged, heartbroken, and suspicious. I made you that way.

"I've also deceived you. I lied to you with words, and even when I wasn't lying with my words, I lied with actions. And I ignored you, giving myself over to this insanity when I had all I really needed right here with you. I know that, as a result, you don't trust me. You probably don't even feel you know me, and I don't blame you. But I'm determined to make you feel, once again, that you really do know who and what I am.

"I won't presume to say I know what you're going through. I know you're hurt, furious, bewildered, and scared, but I don't really know what all of that feels like, because this is a pain I put on you. You didn't put it on me. But please help me understand what you're going through. Tell me what it's like, and I promise I won't run away or defend myself when you tell me. I'll listen, no matter how hard it is to hear it.

"And please try to believe me when I tell you that you can't imagine what I feel either. I've broken the heart of the one person I never wanted to hurt. And because of that, I'm in so much pain—so much self-hate and guilt—and the pain doesn't get better. That's good. I deserve it. But know this: I'll never really get past this. I hope you'll forgive me, but I'll never fully forgive myself. I'll go to my grave regretting this, and years after you've forgiven me, I'll still be asking myself, 'How could you?'

"But I know you need more than words, so here's the plan I'm following. I made a copy of it for you. I'm not asking you to *trust* me. I'm asking you to *watch* me. And as you watch, see if I can't, over a period of time, win back the trust from you that I so miss and crave."

2. Ask her what she needs you to do to help regain her trust and rebuild intimacy in the marriage.

3. Ask her what this has all been like for her, and listen *without interrupting or defending yourself* as she tells you.

4. Ask her if she'll agree to meet with you weekly for thirty minutes. Use these meetings as times for her to update you on how she feels your marriage is progressing and to share any concerns or questions she has. Let this be, primarily, *her* time to express herself to you.

5. Institute a daily habit of praying together and reading a few verses of Scripture together daily, if only for a few minutes. Become the priest in the home who sees to it that, as a family, you devote some time to shared worship and prayer.

6. Close this meeting time with prayer, and thank her again for giving you another chance and for partnering with you after you've hurt her so badly. Show her humility and tenderness, and show them both to her frequently.

7. If your marriage is in immediate danger or if there are still things you need to confess and "come clean" about, read "Marriage" in the appendix.

RATIONALE

You can't make your spouse trust you again, nor can you undo the pain you've caused. But you can help her understand that *you* understand what you've done and what needs to be done about it. That's what restitution and rebuilding are all about.

PRAYER

Father, look on the heart of this woman I love so much but have treated so badly. You have the ability to touch her heart in the places I can no longer touch, and You have the power to restore her confidence in You and in the wonderful qualities You've given her. So by Your grace, heal and undo the hurts I've inflicted on her in my madness. And by that same grace, give her the ability to go on with me, trusting not in me but in You and in Your power to keep even an erring sheep like me from straying again. I ask this in Jesus's name. Amen.

GAME STATUS UPON COMPLETION OF SECTION TWO

By the end of Section Two (Order), you should have done the following: (Check off each item you've completed.)

_____ Incorporated a fifteen-minute daily period that includes Bible reading (one chapter per day), prayer (five minutes), verbal recommitment, and motive review (five minutes).

_____ Defined *sexual sobriety* as abstinence from pornography or immoral contact and begun counting the number of days/weeks/months/years you've been sexually sober.

_____ Contacted an accountability group in your area and decided which night to attend.

_____ Begun planning who to choose as an accountability partner, giving yourself twelve more days to find a partner and begin weekly meetings with him.

_____ Set a time with your wife (if married) to make an acknowledgement, expression, and clarification according to the action plan on Day 12.

If you've left any of these action items undone, go back and complete them before continuing to Section Three.

SECTION THREE

R

Day 13 **The Arena and the Opposition**
*We examine the opposition from the world
and the devil that we're bound to encounter
when we play The Game.*

O

Day 14 **Action Plan for the Arena**

Day 15 **The Wounded Player**
*We examine whatever personal wounds we
may have sustained and learn to deal with
them constructively.*

UNDERSTANDING

Day 16 **Action Plan for Healing**

T

Day 17 **Understanding Temptation**
*We examine the temptations we're bound to
experience and lay the groundwork for
managing them successfully.*

Day 18 **Action Plan for Understanding
Temptation**

E

DAY 13

THE ARENA AND
THE OPPOSITION

You have been given the choice between war and dishonor.
—WINSTON CHURCHILL TO THE BRITISH PARLIAMENT, 1938

Everything was going too well. My prayer life thrived, I craved the Word (taking in at least four chapters every morning), and I was growing under Pastor Chuck Smith's excellent teaching at Calvary Chapel in Southern California. My new friendships also bloomed, sexual temptations were a relatively minor issue, and I'd fallen deeply in love with the beautiful young woman who would, in another two years, become my wife.

I'd been in The Game for a little less than a year, but it seemed more like a honeymoon than a contest. And can any honeymoon last forever?

Not this one. Suddenly, for no clear reason, sexual temptations started hitting me more frequently, and a craving for porn would come at the oddest times. The memories and fantasies I thought I was through with started flooding me again, and I got edgy, temperamental, and moody. My future bride and I started fighting over the most insignificant things; and seemingly out of nowhere, I began feeling old childhood hurts I hadn't felt or even considered for years.

I was sure I must have been doing something wrong, and I told that to my counselor.

"What makes you think that?" he asked.

"Because I was getting so much better! If it's all falling apart, I must be messing up somewhere."

"Uh-huh. And just what did you think the world and the devil were going to do while you kept getting better? Congratulate you with a telegram?"

It had been years since I'd given Satan any real thought, and I'd always thought the us-versus-them mentality many Christians had toward the world was a bit paranoid.

"You've got enemies, Joe," my counselor continued. "Every believer does. And your enemies aren't about to sit back and enjoy your progress."

Then his face took on that look counselors get when they're about to say something they know their client doesn't want to hear. "The fun's over. You want to keep getting better? Great. But freedom's something you fight to *get*, and fight to *keep*. So no, this doesn't mean you're messing up. It only means you're in the arena, like it or not. So fight—or die."

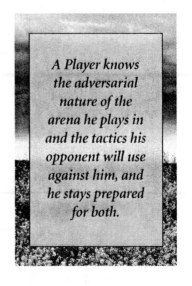

A Player knows the adversarial nature of the arena he plays in and the tactics his opponent will use against him, and he stays prepared for both.

That week, our work turned away from repentance and structure and focused on understanding the nature of the battle I'd gotten myself into.

THE VALUE OF INSIGHT

Understanding—the third part of your five-part process (repentance, order, understanding, training, endurance)—doesn't solve your problems. But it helps you manage them more effectively. To run a business, you need to understand each of its departments; and to be a good steward of your body, you need a basic understanding of nutrition, exercise, and hygiene. Knowing these things, of course, won't make you healthy if you don't apply them. Still, to have something to apply, you've got to acquire some understanding. And that's the value of this part of the process. For the next six days, then, we'll develop a better understanding of the arena (or the environment) in which you're playing The Game, the wounds you may have sustained before playing, and the temptations you'll experience as you play in the future.

Today, our focus will be the arena (the world) and the opposition (the devil) that comes along with it. Our goal is threefold, and it's similar to goals our coaches used to drill into us when we played in high school:

1. Know the field you're playing on.

2. Know your opponent.

3. Know your strategy for dealing with both.

Know the Field You're Playing On

From a biblical perspective, the world is more than the earth. While the earth is the physical globe we exist on, the world is more—it's a multifaceted environment with physical, psychological, and spiritual elements that are at times both wonderful and treacherous.

And it's the treacherous part we'd best be familiar with.

Remember, although God created the world, the world is not the way God created it. It became something else. When Adam sinned, everything in the environment—man, woman, the earth, and the spiritual realm—changed. Read Genesis 3 in its entirety and you see the devastation of paradise lost and the new form the world would take. An ongoing battle would ensue between Satan and Eve's seed (the coming Messiah), a battle with bloody long-term ramifications for all of humanity. Adam and Eve (and thus all husbands and wives) would experience physical pain and relational power struggles, man's work would become hard, the ground itself would be adversarial at times, and everyone would eventually die.

This isn't the world God intended. It became, in fact, an arena in which His people would be called to exist, fight, and conquer.

And much of what we're called to conquer is both subtle and pervasive.

Look at the way the apostle John describes this: "Do not love the world or the things in the world. If anyone loves the world, the love of the Father is not in him. For all that is in the world—the lust of the flesh, the lust of the eyes, and the pride of life—is not of the Father but is of the world" (1 John 2:15–16).

John wrote this, by the way, sometime around AD 90. Even then, he said, the world was a vast celebration of lust. Does anyone really think things have gotten better since then?

This puts you in one heck of a position. You're already beset with any number of sexual thoughts and tendencies that come from within (such as your imaginations, dreams, fantasies, and longings). On top of that, you live in an environment that aggravates the problem by offering open, blatant displays of lust in every conceivable form. The billboards you drive past, the scantily clad women you see in the mall, the sexy newspaper ads, the seductive magazine covers on even the most "respectable" publications—all of these conspire to pull a Player out of The Game and into the pit.

That makes you a bit like a man with asthma who lives in a polluted, smoggy environment. Poor guy—he's got both an internal and external problem. His internal problem is bad enough, but the environment he lives in aggravates it even more!

So does yours. This arena is clearly not your home field. You play here, but your citizenship is elsewhere. It couldn't be in this sexually idolatrous environment, with monuments to erotic gods and goddesses everywhere. Yet these monuments have their dark appeal, and they become the external triggers every serious Player has to contend with. So let's better understand what these triggers are and what you're required to do about them.

External Triggers
Are Environmental and Unavoidable

Every culture has monuments to its deities, so it stands to reason that a sexually idolatrous culture would pay homage to its gods.

And what homage this culture pays! Is there any product or creative endeavor that doesn't use lust to promote itself? You're bombarded daily—hourly, in fact, and maybe even more frequently—with sexual triggers.

A sexual trigger is something external or internal that arouses you sexually, so whatever turns you on qualifies as a trigger. When triggers are external, they're part of the physical environment, appealing to one of your five senses (sight, sound, smell, taste, or touch). Most men get snagged by "sight" triggers, since we're very visual creatures. A person or image that we see, then, can trigger us quickly. Of course, a sexy voice or appealing perfume can arouse our other senses as well, but visuals are usually the snares we trip on.

What's our responsibility, then, if sexual triggers are so common? Does God expect us to reach a point at which they'll no longer tempt us? Or should we all relocate and move to some obscure place where we'll never have to deal with billboards, sexy clothes, or unexpected Super Bowl halftime exposures?

YOUR STRATEGY FOR TRIGGERS: REDUCE AND ACCEPT

Good stewardship, remember, is your goal. So a good steward will *reduce* the triggers in his environment when and where he can. Then, having done so, he'll *accept* the fact that triggers are part of life in this fallen world. He'll view them the way he views the smog: it's a nuisance, but it doesn't have to ruin his life.

So let's forget the broader world—the freeway billboards, sidewalks, and shopping malls—and concentrate instead on your personal section in the arena. Let's look at the magazines you subscribe to, the books you read, the movies you rent, the music you enjoy, and the television shows you watch. Do they present the lifestyle of a serious Player? Remember Paul's thoughts on lifestyle: "All things are lawful for me, but all things are not helpful" (1 Corinthians 6:12).

Indeed, plenty of television shows and movies are legitimate—

meaning, at least, they're not pornographic. But are they helpful? Do you feed your mind and soul with influences that move you along toward your higher goals, or do you binge on mental junk food that doesn't relax you as much as it pollutes you?

Or to put it another way: if I visited your home, would I even *know* that you're a Player? Would the evidence be there, both by what I would and would not see in your environment?

That's the acid test. So have you, as much as possible, reduced the physical triggers in the part of the arena in which you can reduce them (your home, your car, your office)? If not, then you've got homework to do.

But having reduced triggers when and where you can, you've got to accept the presence of the other triggers that will always be part of the broader environment. This has been a hard lesson for me, because I used to stress so badly over the fact that triggers could still arouse me. Every time I'd drive past a suggestive billboard and get turned on, I'd feel like such an unredeemable loser!

I'm learning, I hope, to relax a bit. Hating myself for being tempted doesn't relieve the temptation. But immediate prayer and refocusing do. I'm not, after all, responsible for all the sexual idols this world has erected. If and when they tempt me, that doesn't mean I've sinned. It's what I *do* when I'm tempted that counts.

When you and I stand before the judgment seat of Christ, He's not going to ask us if we reached a point at which we became "temptation-free." He will, though, demand an account of the way we handled temptations when they came. And a special blessing is pronounced on those who handle them well: "Blessed is the man who endures temptation; for when he has been approved, he will receive the crown of life which the Lord has promised to those who love Him" (James 1:12).

So your management goal is to reduce the triggers in your environment when and where you can. Then, having done so, resist the ones that get in your way. There's a crown waiting for you when you do.

KNOW YOUR OPPONENT

When Nehemiah and his men started their work on Jerusalem's walls, their enemies pounced. Sanballat, especially, pulled out a slew of dirty tricks to stop the rebuilding: mockery, humiliation, threats, and inducements to compromise. (Read Nehemiah 4 for the whole story.) John Maxwell, in *The Maxwell Leadership Bible*, has these observations of Sanballat and his tactics: "Soon after the wall around Jerusalem started going up, word reached Sanballat of the construction. He knew that the repair of the wall and the restoration of Jerusalem would bring a major shift in commerce and political power. Sanballat liked the status quo and had a vested interest in Jerusalem remaining in disrepair, so he set about his distracting work."[11]

TO PURSUE GODLINESS IS TO INSTIGATE ADVERSITY

Could the parallels between Sanballat and Satan be any clearer? God has initiated a rebuilding process in you, reestablishing your sexual and spiritual boundaries and restoring you to the man He created you to be.

So Satan pounces. He knows a major restoration of you will bring a shift in commerce. When you compromised, you cooperated with Satan. But now you've stopped cooperating and have become an obstacle to his agenda. That's because every man who becomes a Player becomes an influence for righteousness, which also makes him a hindrance to the god of unrighteousness. Satan, like Sanballat, likes the status quo, and he has a vested interest in your life remaining in disrepair. So naturally, he'll set about his distracting work.

Now let's not give him too much credit. My own history proves that I can sabotage my own life without any help from him, so I'll give him neither credit nor blame for my failures. Sexual sin, after all, is seen in Scripture as a problem of the flesh, not a devil to be cast out.

Still, it's foolish to ignore your opponent's zeal. He hates you, deeply and fervently, and he is committed to undoing every good thing God has initiated in your life. By God's grace, you're rebuilding.

Your enemy knows restoration when he sees it, and he can't wait to tear it down. So mount both a good offense and defense, first by respecting your opponent's commitment to your destruction. Peter said as much when he advised us, "Be sober, be vigilant; because your adversary the devil walks about like a roaring lion, seeking whom he may devour" (1 Peter 5:8). Paul took this even further by commending a good understanding of your opponent's tactics: "lest Satan should take advantage of us; for we are not ignorant of his devices" (2 Corinthians 2:11).

More than ever, your opponent has designs on you. He'll employ every available slime-ball trick to distract you from playing effectively. So in the interest of resisting him, let's look at a few of his tactics.

ACCUSATION

Your opponent loves to *accuse you*, both to God and to yourself. That's his forte. He accused God to Eve when he seduced her (Genesis 3:4–5), then he accused Job before God (Job 1:10–11). Evidently, he likes accusing all of us before God, because in the book of Revelation we see heaven rejoicing when he's finally cast down, and part of the heavenly joy comes from their no longer having to listen to his accusations against us (Revelation 12:10)!

I've always wished Satan acted like Hollywood says he does. If he was as obvious as he is in the movies—say, if he levitated a little girl and made her head spin around—I'd recognize him and his tricks. But he's subtler than that. He speaks to our weaknesses in ways that make us think it isn't him speaking at all. So when he accuses me, I may not even recognize his voice.

When the accusations come—"You're so hopeless; you're such a failure; you've really blown it this time! God's *through* with you!"—that's almost certainly Satan speaking, playing on our insecurities, trying to separate us from the grace of God.

got some structure in place, he sees a very unwelcome wall going up. Now it's hardball time.

So irrational fears full of what-ifs are often nothing more than his threats, hurled at you in hopes of frightening you away from The Game. He's like a gorilla-sized football player, grunting and beating his chest downfield from you, trying to intimidate you. He'd love nothing more than to paralyze you with fear of the unknown and doubts about the future. And often, he'll use your past as a way of predicting (inaccurately, of course) your potential.

You've tried before, perhaps, and failed. Failure carries such a sting that a man may feel, after trying and failing too many times, more comfortable staying where he is, even if he's in a destructive, hopeless place. Rather than risk being disappointed again, he prefers inaction to dashed hopes, and who can blame him? It's awful to realize you've reached and (for the hundredth time!) fallen short. So after experiencing failure too many times, hope seems awfully dangerous.

Enter Satan, playing on that old fear. He'll tell you you're setting yourself up for another disappointment, because you've never stayed clean before. He'll insist you're making promises you'll never keep, adopting habits you'll soon break, and dreaming unattainable dreams. He'll plant this seemingly logical thought in your head: *I'm a fool to think I, of all people, can really change my ways. Teach this old dog some new tricks? Nah, it'll never happen.*

Hey, I know this lie very well. He began shouting it at me twenty-one years ago, and he *still* won't give it a rest! So I'm sure you'll hear it too.

STRATEGY: THE SWORD OF THE WORD

If you want to play well, emulate the champions. No champion conquered an opponent more decidedly than Christ conquered Satan, so let's see how He dealt with His opponent's tactics and adopt His approach as our own.

When Satan tempted Jesus in Matthew 4:1–10, he did so when the Lord was weakened from a forty-day fast. How like Satan to attack when his opponent was weary, and don't kid yourself—if he did it to

Christ, he'll do it to you! But when he tried his tactics on Jesus, you'll notice the Lord didn't even bother with a discussion. Instead, He used the Word—and the Word only!—when resisting the devil.

There's the key. This is one of many reasons I harp on the need to be in the Word daily. Because when it comes to doing spiritual battle, you can't draw on weapons you aren't familiar with. But the more you read, study, and commit Scripture to heart, the more effective your arsenal will be when you need it.

And you will need it, because tyrants don't give up easily. As I write this chapter, Iraq just held its first election. I've been over-joyed watching news footage of Iraqi citizens in the new democ-racy, casting ballots with triumph etched into their faces. But this freedom wasn't easily won, and the battle isn't over. The insurgent forces are still terrorizing and killing their own countrymen just to keep them from claiming their new liberties. Tyrants don't grant freedom; it has to be wrestled from them.

You can wrestle your freedom from Satan by knowing and quot-ing the Word, as did Jesus. Much of your battle will be fought in the mind, so a thoughtful quoting of Scripture will take you far. Your job in this spiritual battle is to recognize, respond, and resist.

RECOGNIZE

You must first *recognize* Satan's tactics. Granted, it's hard to know if a thought is coming from Satan or yourself. Weird, negative ideas can come from our own imagination, so let's not go looking for the devil every time we have one.

Still, the Word tells us he's there, he hates us, and he *is* trying to trip us up with accusations, insinuations, and threats (1 Peter 5:8). So if you're getting bombarded with accusative thoughts about your "worthlessness" or "hopelessness," or with suspicions about the people closest to you, or with irrational fears about the future, that's probably your opponent trying to sabotage your rebuilding.

RESPOND

Next, *respond* to your opponent's thrusts with scriptural truth. When he accuses you of being hopeless and beyond grace, answer with the Word (and *think* about what you're saying!): "There is therefore now no condemnation to those who are in Christ Jesus" (Romans 8:1).

When he attempts to divide you from others by whispering insinuations about them, answer with the Word: "[These things] are an abomination to Him . . . a false witness who speaks lies, and one who sows discord among brethren" (Proverbs 6:16, 19).

When he plants doubts in your mind about whether there is any hope for your future, answer with the Word: "Being confident of this very thing, that He who has begun a good work in you will complete it until the day of Jesus Christ" (Philippians 1:6).

It can't be overemphasized: be a man of the Word! Learn it, utilize it as the most effective of all arsenals, and if need be, get past your self-consciousness about speaking it out loud. Because the Word is the most effective response to your opponent's lies.

RESIST

Finally, *resist* the temptation to consider his lies, and thereby you'll resist him. What good, after all, comes from chatting with the devil? You're certainly not going to convert him! So when you've said whichever scripture is appropriate, end the conversation. James put it well: "Resist the devil and he will flee from you" (4:7).

If after answering him with the Word, you refuse to entertain the endless what-ifs and accusations he throws at you, you'll notice the power of those accusations and doubts will diminish. It's not some sort of magic; rather, it's a sound biblical principle. Truth shuts up the father of lies, firmly and effectively.

Paul described this well to the Corinthians: "For the weapons of our warfare are not carnal but mighty in God . . . casting down arguments and every high thing that exalts itself against the knowledge of God, bringing every thought into captivity to the obedience of Christ" (2 Corinthians 10:4–5).

So there's the arena, and that's your opponent. Arenas, you know, have an intense history. Gladiators fought in them, often to the death, and bloodshed was the norm. So yes, The Game gets intense—sometimes so intense the idea of going AWOL has a real appeal. War, whether national, internal, or spiritual, is still war. And war is hell. At times we'd all rather pass.

But Winston Churchill had something to say about passing up conflict when he berated the British Parliament for adopting an appeasement policy toward Hitler after he invaded Czechoslovakia. Parliament hoped that if they left Hitler alone, he'd return the favor. Churchill wasn't nearly so shortsighted, and he scolded them: "You have been given the choice between war and dishonor. You have chosen dishonor; now you will have both!"

Sure, being a player can be exhausting, hurtful, and heartbreaking. Sometimes the skirmishes The Game requires seem too much or too long, making appeasement look awfully good.

But you've already come too far to entertain options like that. If we can honorably avoid a fight, let's do it. But if it's a choice between war and dishonor, let us never, never choose dishonor.

DAY 14

ACTION PLAN FOR THE ARENA

KEY VERSE

Blessed be the LORD my Rock, who trains my hands for war, and my fingers for battle.

—PSALM 144:1

PRINCIPLE

To play (and fight) successfully, you've got to know the playing field (the arena), your opponent's tactics, and your own strategies for dealing with both. This is required for good stewardship, strong performance, and successful fighting.

ACTION

Write or type into your own computer the answers to the following questions.

1. What kind of external triggers in the environment usually affect you? Remember, external triggers are physical, so thoughts and fantasies don't count. These can include people, billboards, magazine covers—anything in the physical realm that triggers you sexually.

2. Under what circumstances—when and where—do you usually encounter these triggers?

3. Can you find ways to avoid them in the future? If so, how?

4. What external triggers could be reduced in your home, your car, or your place of business? Be brutally honest about this by examining your forms of entertainment and lifestyle with an eye toward what is helpful in moving you toward your goals.

5. Since your opponent is watching you as your walls are being built, what sort of accusations, lies, or threats do you think he is throwing at you?

6. How would you answer each of these lies, accusations, or threats? What scripture(s) would you use?

7. Read about spiritual warfare in Ephesians 6:12–17. Which parts of the spiritual armor have you been neglecting? Commit prayerfully to pay attention to those in the future.

RATIONALE

To become a good steward, you have to learn self-management. By asking and answering these questions, you are examining your lifestyle more carefully. These questions also force you to consider the tactics your opponent may be using against you, and they better prepare you to resist those tactics in the future.

PRAYER

Father, I'm quickly graduating from prodigal, to child, to Player, and now, to warrior. I know The Game is at times deadly earnest, and I refuse to say no to its challenges and demands. But the more I consider the nature of both the arena and my opponent, I have to admit my fears. Both seem larger and stronger than me; both are more committed to my destruction than I've been to my life and health.

Yet we're winning, You and I. I rejoice in that and ask only that You remind me that You always go with me into the arena, never leaving me alone or ill equipped. Increase my faith in Your consistency, and thereby take my eyes off my own weakness as I approach the arena.

For I approach it as a grateful Player who wants to please his Coach. Grant that I may. I ask this in Jesus's name. Amen.

DAY 15

THE WOUNDED PLAYER

Sometimes one has simply to endure a period of depression
for what it may hold of illumination, if one can live
through it, attentive to what it exposes or demands.

—MAY SARTON

There was no more putting it off—I had to see the dentist.

I'd avoided him for months, even though my left lower tooth was hurting so badly it brought me to tears. I knew if I saw the dentist he'd tell me I had a cavity, and I'd never had one before. So the idea of a drill and a needle in my mouth scared me away from the help I needed, until finally the pain became unbearable.

"Congratulations, Joe," he smiled. "You not only have your first cavity, but you've let this go for so long, your decay has reached your gum line. Now you need more than a filling. You need a root canal."

> *A Player is a steward of his emotions, so he addresses them by attending to his wounds through honesty and forgiveness.*

He recommended I make an appointment for surgery. Of course, I didn't. I did, though, discover an over-the-counter product called Anbesol, which, when swabbed over my tooth, effectively numbed the pain and thereby allowed me to go on ignoring the problem.

Within months, I lost the tooth entirely. By using Anbesol, I had killed the pain that was trying to draw my attention to the problem. And by ignoring the problem, I had only damaged myself further.

The medication I used on my wound became the very thing that kept it from healing. If I'd only been willing to address the pain head-on, I'd still have the tooth.

"Please, No Touchy-Feely!"

I can almost hear you saying it. We're about to discuss emotional wounds, and you're afraid I'm going to ask you to go curl up in a corner and cry your little eyes out because your second-grade classmates laughed at your orange sweater.

Relax. I'm not into that.

I'm leery of the "touchy-feely" approach toward dealing with emotional pain. Self-pity never advanced any man's maturity, and I find it downright spooky when guys seem a little *too* anxious to cry.

Still, wounds exist, and plenty of Players carry them into the arena. To play well, you have to be aware of your wounds and, if necessary, take care of them. For that reason, we'll spend some time discussing emotional wounds, their role in sexual sin, and the best ways to deal with them.

The Nature of Emotional Wounds

Let's define emotional wounds as past injuries of the soul that still show themselves, either in current pain or current behavior.

They can show themselves in current pain through memories that just won't die. Sometimes a mental picture of a traumatic event—a childhood humiliation or tragedy, for example—keeps intruding into your thoughts. Maybe you let yourself relive it, and all the pain of the event comes flooding back, reopening the sore and making it worse.

Or you may relive the event mentally, but then, in your imagination, you put a different ending on it. That's a common little mind game. You have a fantasy about the past—something emotionally hurtful that to this day you wish you'd handled differently—but in your fantasy, you rewrite history by putting a happier ending on it, usually making yourself the winner or the hero. (Come on, you haven't done that at least once?)

Those sorts of recurring thoughts or daydreams often mean there's a wound that's still festering. If it wasn't, you wouldn't keep thinking about it.

A wound can also show itself in your behavior when it affects the way you relate. Wounds—early rejections, disappointments, or traumas—can become the root of adult isolation, fear of intimacy, a craving for power, or extreme passivity and dependency. In those cases, the wound affects a man's ability to love and trust.

So what's all this got to do with sexual purity, sobriety, and The Game? Well, often (though not always) a man's sexual sin isn't just the result of lust. It might also indicate a problem of love or, more specifically, a problem of *relating*. And at the root of that problem, there's often a wound that he's been medicating with his sexual sin. The sin is a problem, for sure. He's got to repent of it. But it's also been his Anbesol—his way of numbing the pain from his wound—so when he repents and stops using his painkiller, the wound may start hurting more than ever.

And that's exactly what needs to happen. Now he can do something constructive about it, instead of ignoring or medicating it.

Maybe you never thought of sexual sin as medication, but doesn't it often serve the same purpose? When a man anticipates a sexual act, he experiences a pleasant chemical arousal and a fixation on the upcoming act. That's distracting and exhilarating. The more he anticipates, the "higher" he gets. While buying the porn or beginning the foreplay or driving to the strip bar, the excitement grows almost unbearable. Then comes the act itself, and the man drowns in the visuals, the hyperstimulation, the orgasm, and release. It's quite a "fix."

Often, the fix is used just as alcohol and cocaine are used: as a way to forget, numb, or be distracted from unwelcome reality and pain. In that case, sexual sin isn't just sexual. It's anesthetic.

So why would a man keep pumping anesthesia into himself? It's the pleasure principle: pursue pleasure, and avoid pain. This is a lesson we taught ourselves as kids, and we've reinforced it most of our lives. When we're uncomfortable, we reach for something—the remote, a beer, food, a cigarette, a magazine—anything to enhance pleasure and reduce discomfort.

One of the earliest things we learned to reach for was our penis. You probably discovered this as an infant, long before you had any idea what sex was. The hypersensitive male organ is so easily aroused that the slightest touch floods you with comfort, ecstasy, distraction, and excitement. Once you found "the good spot," you learned that when you're bored or uncomfortable, touching yourself there brings immediate, though temporary, relief. And as if that wasn't enough, when you hit puberty and started having orgasms, the good spot probably became a tried-and-true pain reliever.

Over the years, then, there's a good chance you've taught yourself that sexual pleasure is not only enjoyable but an effective painkiller as well. And if you're a man with a significant amount of emotional pain, that's an appealing product. I've worked with homosexual clients, for example, who said a man's embrace helped alleviate the pain they felt over the father who rejected them. Others have confided that when losing themselves in Internet pornography, they created an imaginary world of beautiful women who adored them, and that eased the pain of earlier female rejections.

Men who've been injured by abusive relationships have admitted to me that they have no interest in any kind of intimacy with anyone. They'll just opt for pleasure, because intimacy's too dangerous. Sexual sin is tailor-made for guys like that.

If this is true of you, then by now your wounds may be showing themselves more than ever. Because when you repented, you separated yourself from your painkiller, so the old hurt you've been medicating may resurface. Many guys who aren't willing to deal with their pain simply give up on The Game at this point, not because abandoning sexual sin is so hard but because facing their own pain is too threatening.

But you're not one of those guys. You're a serious Player, and Players identify and deal with their injuries. Of course, that doesn't mean all players are injured, right? So let's put this concept of "wounding" in perspective.

We've all sustained physical injuries. I can show you my scars, you can regale me with accounts of your broken bones, and we can laugh about them, shrug, and move on. No big deal.

Unless you've been *significantly* injured, as some men have. In that case, your past injury will flare up painfully at times, affecting the way you operate and feel. Even though the injury is in the past, the pain it causes is very much in the present. And that's nothing to shrug off.

Likewise, we've all sustained emotional injuries. I can tell you about the girl who wouldn't go steady with me, you can tell me about the sixth grader who bullied you, and we can laugh about it, shrug, and move on. No big deal.

Unless you've been *significantly* injured emotionally, as some men have. In that case, your past injury will flare up, affecting your ability to relate and function. And that, too, is nothing to shrug off.

If that's the case, you're a Wounded Player. When your wound hurts you, you'll be tempted to medicate it with the tried-and-true sexual sin you used in the past. This is what I'd call an internal and nonerotic trigger, because it comes from discomfort, not just sexual arousal. And while it's great that you repented of your sins, you really can't repent of your wounds. They're still there, and they need to be dealt with.

Dealing with your wounds does not mean blaming others, feeling sorry for yourself, making excuses, playing the victim, or making an appearance on *Jerry Springer.* Nor does it mean pretending the wounds don't exist. So what's a Wounded Player to do? Four things: identify, address, release, and relate.

IDENTIFY THE WOUND

Does the very thought of a certain person—or the mention of that person's name—flood you with fear, rage, or sadness?

Is there someone you avoid whenever possible because the idea of interacting with him or her puts you into a panic?

Do you indirectly punish someone—a family member, perhaps, or a former friend—with silence, sarcasm, or gossip?

If so, then you have a wound associated with that person.

Usually the wound is made up of a series of events that happened between you and this person, a few of which especially stand out. And usually, the person involved is someone you were close to—a family member or friend—so he could hurt you at the deepest levels.

After the hurt came the anger that, for whatever reason, you didn't express. Maybe you couldn't. With an abusive father, for example, a boy can hardly express his rage at Dad's cruelty if he knows Dad will retaliate in even more cruel ways. So the wound stays open and raw, then it gets infected with bitterness, which always comes with anger that has nowhere to go.

This is exactly why Jesus said to address a problem directly and immediately: "If your brother sins against you, rebuke him; and if he repents, forgive him" (Luke 17:3).

When you've been wronged, although you're commanded to forgive, you're also commanded to be honest about the wrongdoing. If you aren't, you'll feel unresolved about it, and that lack of resolution easily gives way to resentment. This, of course, makes the wound worse, as the boy who's angry is now also infected with a poisonous combination of bitterness, hurt, fear of expressing his hurt, and (often) disgust with himself for being so afraid.

In some cases—many cases, actually—the kid sees no way out. Maybe his wound was caused by a poor relationship in the home or by peer rejection, physical or sexual abuse, or some ongoing humiliation he had to endure. He believes he can't fight back. Usually, he's right.

But it's not just the pain that affects the boy. It's also the wound's *message*. The message is the interpretation he puts on the event: "If Dad rejected me, it's because I'm an unlovable sissy" or, "If the kids don't like me, it's because everything about me is wrong." And that message will profoundly affect the choices he

n and heal you. Because wounds are generally not healed
attain, and maintain, healthy intimacy.

st clinical supervisor told me to remember that when
came to me for counseling, that person was there because
g went wrong in his or her relationships. And, he stressed,
olution would come not through analysis but through
When people learned to develop strong ties with healthy,
ends and family, they would heal.

e years, I'd have to say he got it right. If you're a Wounded
u're someone who's probably been hiding from the very
craved. Of course, the Anbesol is a painkiller, but it's not
medication, and there's a difference. One simply kills the
other heals the wound.

ur wound, then, first to God. Offer it up; ask Him to help
with it. Confess any bitterness you've allowed yourself to
, and ask for the grace and wisdom to address the wound.
o to the source, if possible. Talk it out; clear the air.
elease the source, whether or not you've been able to talk
ther. And if the old pain resurfaces, make a habit of releas-
oon as you're aware of it. Here's a trick I learned years ago,
o trick at all. Jesus advised it when He said, "Bless those
e you, do good to those who hate you, and pray for those
fully use you" (Matthew 5:44).

ver I remember someone's sin against me, whether in the
ast or the here and now, I try to pray for that person.
ly, I pray God's blessings on his life and His correction of
his life that needs correcting. In doing so, I'm released
burden of hating him, thinking ill of him, obsessing over
use who, in the long run, is punished by my bitterness?
ut me, and I've quite selfishly decided I'd rather not pun-
f any longer.

tly hope you won't either.

makes later in life, the way he relates to people, and the kind of
people to whom he chooses to relate.

In any case, he usually won't assert himself and confront the
wrongdoers. So he manages life as best he can, avoiding the painful
relationship when possible and finding other ways—often sinful,
frequently sexual—to ease his pain. Hence he discovers both the
wound and the "cure," which is no cure at all.

ADDRESS THE PROBLEM

If this comes close to describing your history with a person you've
experienced a deep wound with, then you need to address it. To do
so, ask yourself four questions:

First, is this person *accessible*? (In other words, is he or she alive
and able to be located?)

Second, is a conversation about this *feasible*? That can be a
tough call, because there are plenty of reasons it may not be feasible. He or she may be very old or very ill, and in either case a conversation about past problems isn't feasible. Maybe he's not open
to an honest conversation, or maybe you haven't spoken in so
many years that addressing old business seems out of the question.

Often a conversation with the person *is* feasible, though. You
may still see this person at times, and the wound is still a painful
wall between the two of you. If so, move ahead with plans to
address it.

Third, is your perception of this person and what happened
between the two of you *accurate*? Don't be too quick to say yes. Of
course, if you were abused or violated, there's no question the person was wrong in the extreme. But often, a boy grows up deciding
he's been wronged without considering how he might have mis-
read the situation. In that case, he's not only judged the person's
behavior, but he's also judged the person's motives and character.
(As in, "She hurt me, so everything about her is evil, and everything about our relationship was horrible.") So take some time to
prayerfully, honestly look again at your history.

Fourth, what do you want to *say* to this person? What questions do you still have? What do you want him to know about you and the way you feel? What, if anything, do you want to see changed in your current relationship with this person? In addressing these questions, you're finally getting some resolution and clarity, which is a way of cleaning out the old wound.

If your wound is associated with someone who's still accessible, and if addressing it with him or her seems feasible, then do so. And do it soon. (Tomorrow's action plan will cover some of the mechanics involved.) This is a sensitive, vital part of The Game. Since most emotional wounds are caused by problems between people, it's necessary to address those problems in order to move on and play effectively.

But if the person is not accessible or if it's unfeasible to have such an honest talk, then move directly on to the next step, which is release.

RELEASE THE WOUNDER AND THE WOUND

If you're able to talk out an old problem with someone who's hurt you, you should. But even if you can't, you're still mandated to forgive. Jesus offered no wiggle room on the matter: "If you do not forgive men their trespasses, neither will your Father forgive your trespasses" (Matthew 6:15).

One of my chief criticisms of modern psychology is that it often emphasizes confrontation without forgiveness. People are encouraged to confront whoever has wronged them, get out the anger, and (too often) wallow in either self-righteousness or victimhood. But invariably, the person doesn't move on and heal.

On the other hand, if forgiving means forgetting the thing happened or feeling no pain whatsoever about it, then many of us will never be able to forgive! Fortunately, the biblical concept of forgiveness is something different. The Greek word Jesus used for "forgive" is *aphiemi*, meaning to let go of a debt by not demanding it.[12]

Martin Luther King Jr. had a good take on this: "Forgiveness does not mean ignoring what has been done or putting a false label

on an evil act. It means, rather, that t[...] as a barrier to the relationship."

When you release someone who's [...] right to punish that person. You relin[...] in the past to "hurt him back"—the s[...] casm, or hurtful remarks—and you [...] acid that's been welling up whenever [...]

There are practical reasons for th[...] you rarely hurt the person you're not [...] person remains blissfully unaware of [...] tainly not hurting him. Or if the pers[...] in the past, it's likely he wouldn't ca[...] angry you are. This is harsh but true: i[...] one who's been relentlessly hurtful [...] wouldn't have been so hurtful in the [...] think he loses sleep when we don't fo[...]

In other words, exactly who do we [...] Besides which, there are some thin[...] judging is one of them. Which is exac[...] long-term punishment to Him: "Be[...] selves, but rather give place to wrath [...] is Mine, I will repay,' says the Lord" ([...]

If the wounder is unrepentant, unw[...] indifferent to the pain he's caused you [...] for him that's worse than anything yo[...] you've got a life to live and a Game t[...] you to allow someone's sin to keep dis[...] matters?

When you release the wounder, yo[...] tive, crippling feelings that weaken y[...] forgiveness.

NOW REL[...]

The key to dealing with emotional p[...] source if possible, forgive, and the[...]

strengthe[...] unless we[...]

My fi[...] someone [...] somethin[...] the real [...] intimacy.[...] loving fri[...]

Over t[...] Player, yo[...] thing he's[...] a healing [...] pain; the [...]

Take y[...] you deal [...] hold on t[...]

Then [...] Then [...] it out tog[...] ing it as s[...] which is [...] who curs[...] who spite[...]

When[...] distant p[...] Specifica[...] any sin i[...] from the [...] him. Bec[...] No one b[...] ish mysel[...]

I ferve[...]

DAY 16

ACTION PLAN FOR HEALING

KEY VERSE

The Spirit of the LORD is upon Me, because He has anointed Me to preach the gospel to the poor; He has sent Me to heal the broken-hearted.

—LUKE 4:18

PRINCIPLE

Because human relationships often go wrong, they can be the source of tremendous pain. We need intimacy, but when intimate relations have been a source of pain, then the thing we've needed becomes the experience that has wounded us the most deeply. The wounds, often sustained early in life, create pain that a Player may have medicated through sexual sin. When he abandons the sin, the pain may then reemerge and require attention.

ACTION

1. Take a minute to think seriously about any person who comes to mind when you think of wounds. Is there a relationship that, to this day, you remember with intense feelings of anger or fear? If so, write down or type into your computer the following:

   a. The person's name and the type of relationship you had with him or her (father, girlfriend, brother, classmate, and so on).

b. List the reasons the memory of this person is still painful. Specifically, what did he or she do that caused you pain? (Give at least two examples.)

c. How did you respond to this person (avoided, fought back, hid from, pleaded with, and so on)?

d. How did this relationship affect the way you now relate to others?

e. Has sexual sin had any role in medicating the pain over this relationship?

f. Is this person still a part of your life? If so, is he or she accessible?

g. Is an honest conversation with this person feasible?

h. If so, what would you like to say to this person today?

If this person is accessible and it's feasible to discuss this, block out a time within the next five days in which you'll call, write, or e-mail him or her, requesting some time to talk. Sample communication: "I've been thinking a lot lately about our relationship and things that happened between us. I'd really like to clear the air and have an honest talk. Does that sound reasonable to you? When and where can we meet to do this?"

2. Set a date and time to discuss this, preferably face to face. (If it's a long-distance relationship, obviously you'll have to go with a phone conversation.) Before meeting, prayerfully reconsider the way you've viewed the relationship. Try to see it from his perspective, and allow that both your memory and your perceptions are imperfect. Keep that in mind when you talk.

3. When you meet, tell him the following:

a. What happened between the two of you that still hurts to this day.

b. How what happened between you affected the way you relate to God and others.

c. Ask if you might have it wrong. Are you remembering correctly? Does he remember it differently? Did you also hurt or disappoint him? Listen carefully and respectfully to his responses.

d. Tell him what you'd like your relationship to be like now, if possible.

e. Ask his forgiveness if in any way you've offended or hurt him in the past.

f. If he shows either indifference or hostility to you during this conversation, then let him know you're only trying to clear things up; and if that's not possible, you still wish him well and won't impose yourself any further.

g. Make sure to thank him for discussing this with you. Tell him you know he didn't have to, and you respect his willingness to be honest with you.

4. Begin praying specifically, and daily, for the person who is the source of your wound. Ask for God's grace in that person's life, for the correcting of sin, and for his salvation if the person is not a believer.

5. If you can't take any action on this because of the other party's inability or unwillingness to address it with you, or if you're still experiencing a significant amount of pain or confusion over your wound, then consider speaking with either your pastor or a Christian counselor. If you opt for a counselor, get a referral from your pastor or from someone you know. The value of ongoing counseling will be in the counselor's ability to help you decide how to best deal with both your ongoing pain and the relationship that's been the source of it.

RATIONALE

If you've sustained a serious emotional wound, it will go on hindering you as you try to move ahead in sobriety, purity, and service. You'll also find yourself more tempted than ever to return to the sin you've used as medication in the past. So it's vital that you address the issue head-on, first through honest discussion and then through prayerful forgiveness and release.

PRAYER

Father, I've had this pain so long, I can't imagine life without it. I've been hurt, and I know, in many ways, I've caused hurt as well. There are people whose actions I still don't understand, and at times, I've even blamed You for not protecting me from their madness. But I know You're just and cannot be blamed. So help me to love as You've commanded me to love. Give me the courage to confront my wounds, discuss them honestly, consider my own part in them, forgive, and develop the relations of love and support I know You're calling me to. Give me the courage to face my wounds; give me the maturity never to wallow in them. I ask this in Jesus's name. Amen.

UNDERSTANDING TEMPTATION

I am tempted to think that I am now an established Christian, that I have overcome this or that lust so long, so that there is no fear of temptation. This is a lie of Satan. One might as well speak of gunpowder reaching a point at which it can no longer catch fire.

—ROBERT MURRAY M'CHEYNE

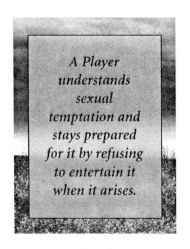

A Player understands sexual temptation and stays prepared for it by refusing to entertain it when it arises.

The subject was purity, the television show was live, and I was the last guest to come on. I'd watched the others being interviewed before me, and their stories were wonderful. They'd all lived pretty healthy, normal lives; and each wanted to testify that, yes, it was possible to stay pure in an impure world, because they were living proof.

I was next. The host introduced me, commented on my work, and then wanted my testimony.

He soon looked as though he was sorry he'd asked. As I told my story, the contrast between my life and the other guests' was like comparing snow and sludge.

"But, Joe," he said, obviously hoping to put a nice ending on it, "looking at you today, it's clear you're beyond all that. You're God's man now, delivered and victorious. Why, I'll bet you could never be tempted toward that stuff again, could you?"

Long pause. I knew what he wanted to hear; I also knew the truth. I finally broke the awkward silence with an explanation: "I wish I could say temptation's not part of my life, but it's there. I *am* victorious, not because I'm temptation free, but because, by the grace of God, I know what to do when those temptations come."

It wasn't the ideal answer, and it certainly got no applause. But it was real. And *real* always gets you further than *ideal*.

TEMPTATION HAPPENS

Remember, your primary goal is to attain, and then maintain, sexual sobriety. You attain it through repentance and then maintain it through vigilance. You've got be watchful enough to recognize temptations when they come, because your ability to manage them will determine your success or failure in protecting your sobriety. On Day 19, we'll start practicing temptation-resistance techniques. But for now, we'll examine the hows and whys of temptation and clarify what you're expected to do when tempted. Let's begin by breaking down the terms we use when referring to sexual temptations.

SEXUAL AROUSAL

You're a sexual creature, and as such, you can be sexually aroused. You're not trying to become *non*sexual. You're trying instead to stay sexually *responsible*. Sexual purity isn't an absence of sexual response; it's a responsible approach toward sex.

"Sexual" describes several things about you. You have sexual desires, sexual organs, and sexual thoughts, responses, and capabilities. Put together, they create in you a desire to connect, both emotionally and physically. That's not only normal; it's intentional.

The first negative thing God said about man in the Scripture touches on this: "The LORD God said, 'It is not good that man should be alone; I will make him a helper . . .'" (Genesis 2:18). Then, having done so, He commanded Adam and Eve to have a sexual relationship (that must've been a tough one to obey) and pronounced strong approval on all He'd created, their sexual union included: "Then God blessed them, and God said to them, 'Be fruitful and multiply' . . . Then God saw everything that He had made, and indeed it was very good" (Genesis 1:28, 31).

You're not playing The Game to solve the problem of being sexual, because being sexual is *not* a problem. You're playing because your sexuality, like all parts of your life, is marred by the Fall. As soon as sin entered, it corrupted all of man's existence: his relationships, work life, and sexuality. Which leads to the many problems associated with what we could call "fallen sexuality."

SEXUAL LUST

Lust means literally to covet, strongly desire, or set your heart on something. Technically, the word can apply to both legitimate and illegitimate desires, but it's generally used in the negative sense (as in "lusting after a married woman"). When you lust sexually, then, you allow yourself to desire what's not rightfully yours.

I don't view my desire for my wife as "lust." Our sexual union is legitimized, so when I desire her, I'm not coveting anything I'm not rightfully entitled to. If I covet another person sexually, though, then I'm lusting, because I'm setting my heart on something I've no right to.

Lust is an internal sin—serious, though not necessarily acted on. It's also a sin plenty of men engage in because it produces a pleasant buzz, a chemical response that's both exciting and comforting, which is why guys often like ogling attractive women. They're not just appreciating physical beauty. They're also enjoying the high they get from lusting.

SEXUAL ACTING OUT

When you "act out," you physically express what you're internally experiencing. So if you're steaming mad at someone and hold it in, you're enraged but not acting on it. If you act out, you punch the guy. The same is true of sexual acting out. When you commit a sinful sexual act, you've transgressed by physically expressing the sin you were entertaining inwardly.

I want you to have these concepts down because they help you monitor your sobriety. Remember, sexual sobriety is the standard of behavior you require of yourself. Sexual purity is the ideal you constantly strive for. You'll fall short of the ideal at times; the standard is something you can't afford to fall short of. So keep these three points in mind:

First, sexual *arousal* is neither a sin nor a violation of sobriety. When it occurs within marriage, it's legitimate. If an unmarried man is sexually aroused, what he does with that arousal is what determines whether or not he's sinned.

Second, sexual *lust* (the coveting of someone you're not entitled to) is a sin, but not a breaking of sobriety unless the use of pornography is involved. If you lust, you do have to confess it in prayer and commit to not indulging in it. Just because it doesn't constitute breaking sobriety, that doesn't mean it isn't serious.

Third, sexual *acting out* does constitute breaking sobriety. If you use pornography or act out with another individual, that's a relapse, which means you've lost your sobriety and need to begin building it again.

As a Player, you'll be tempted to sexually lust and sexually act out. Your temptations come from three primary sources:

TEMPTATIONS FROM WITHIN

James said, "But each one is tempted when he is drawn away by his own desires and enticed" (James 1:14). That's not to say it's a sin to be tempted; rather, it means it's because we are sinful creatures that we can be tempted. So a man can be tempted to daydream about past sexual experiences or images he's seen, or he can of his own volition look at erotic images.

TEMPTATIONS FROM SATAN

The devil does, indeed, tempt and entice. He tempted Jesus, beguiled Eve, and put it into Judas Iscariot's heart to betray Christ. So naturally he'll work on you, trying to influence you into something attractive and lethal.

TEMPTATION FROM OTHERS

Temptations offered from others can be the hardest to deal with. When you know a potential partner is willing, tearing yourself away is a challenge. Just ask Joseph, whose boss's wife kept coming on to him (Genesis 39). Or Bathsheba, who got propositioned by Israel's handsome King David (see Day 3). People can and will, at times, impose strong temptations on you.

Those three primary sources will always be there, by the way. Your own capacity for lust—your thoughts, memories, and weaknesses—won't disappear. And Satan and other people certainly aren't going anywhere. Temptation will always be a fact of life that a wise person will accept and be prepared for.

How often or hard your temptations come is not what really matters. What *does* matter is your response to them, so let's clarify the options you have when you're tempted.

STIMULATION: OPPORTUNITY KNOCKS

Temptation begins with stimulation. That happens when something from within you (a thought, memory, or longing) or an external trigger (something or someone in the environment) appeals to you. It basically presents itself as an option or an invitation.

Poor Joseph had the option thrown in his face several times when Potiphar's wife kept blatantly inviting him to lie with her. King David had the option presented when he spotted a beautiful woman bathing. The option presented itself to me when I saw an adult bookstore with its front door invitingly opened. And you? I'm sure you've had your share. Anytime a situation presents itself, giving you the opportunity to lust or act out, that's stimulation. And when stimulated, you make a decision.

Think of stimulation as a door-to-door salesman. He knocks. You look through your peephole and see him standing there with his briefcase, and you make a decision: "I will or I will not answer the door."

It's easier, isn't it, to make that decision right away, before he gets a chance to engage you in his sales pitch?

This is a source of tension between my wife and me, because I'm not a good customer for door-to-door salesmen. When I see one coming, I usually don't open the door when he knocks, preferring instead to yell, "Not interested!" through the (firmly) closed front door. And if by chance one of them catches me off guard and I do answer his knock, the moment I see who he is and what he wants, I cut him off with, "Thanks, not interested, bye!" as I close the door.

I know that's not the friendliest approach, but it saves me a lot of aggravation, because I know the goal of a salesman is to get his foot in the door. Once he does, I'll be stuck listening to a long pitch, after which I'll have to explain and defend my reasons for not wanting to buy.

My beautiful Renee, though, is a kinder and finer person than her husband. She opens the door to salesmen, listens politely to their spiel, and gives them her full attention even though she has no intention of buying anything. It's just not in her nature to cut somebody off.

And don't think for a minute the salesman can't spot a nice person when he sees one! He takes full advantage of her kindness, pulling out every guilt trip and appeal he knows to manipulate her into a purchase, until I finally interrupt, stepping between them and wishing the man a nice day as I close the door a little too loudly.

She always reproaches me for hurting his feelings; I always

plead with her to leave the door closed. "Because," I say when she asks why, "it's hard to get rid of them once you answer, so next time, don't!"

There's your goal—don't answer when stimulation knocks. It's not that hard to do this, if you do it during the first part of the stimulation phase.

Let's take an everyday temptation as an example. You're driving to work, stopped at a traffic signal, and an attractive woman crosses the street in front of you. You glance through the windshield and notice she's gorgeous and not too modestly dressed; the opportunity to look, lust, and possibly even flirt is knocking.

Whether you realize it or not, you're making a decision: "I will or I will not answer the door."

If you decide quickly *not* to answer, you'll tear your eyes away from her without too much effort. But the longer you wait to decide, the harder it gets to decide properly. And, in fact, by not deciding, you *have* decided. Because when you don't decide to resist the opportunity, you do decide to entertain it.

Entertainment: a Slippery Slope

It's possible to disentangle yourself from a salesman, even if you do open the door. But if you take it a step further and let him in the house, you're in trouble. He'll push harder once he's inside; you'll get worn down with each passing minute, your judgment will slip, and (unless you really *do* need the product) you'll probably make the wrong decision by giving in to him.

Once you let the stimulation inside, that's what happens. And that's entertainment.

When you decide not to resist the stimulation by continuing to look it over, your ability to detach from it gets worn down. That's because stimulation, once it gives way to lust, quickly becomes obsession.

It's easy to visualize how King David's attraction to Bathsheba probably evolved.

First look: "Wow, she's beautiful. Should I look again?"

Second look: "She's incredible. Hmm. I'm alone; her husband's probably in the battle; she's available. Should I go for it?"

Third look: "I *have* to have her. Nothing else matters."

Something scary happened to this good man's judgment between the first and second look—a consideration. The first look simply identified the woman as attractive. He decided then and there whether or not he'd indulge in a second look.

The second look, I'll bet, involved a consideration—"Should I or shouldn't I go for it?" No doubt his heart pumped; he got aroused; his imagination raced. After that, it was full speed ahead: "Nothing else matters."

That's the obsessive nature of the entertainment phase. Once your lust is inflamed, judgment falters and then fades. Indulgence—acting out the lust that's been inflamed—is a short step away.

James said as much when he described lust, action, and consequences: "But each one is tempted when he is drawn away by his own desires and enticed. Then, when desire has conceived [second look], it gives birth to sin; and sin, when it is full-grown, brings forth death" (James 1:14–15).

MANAGEMENT GOAL: STOP AT STIMULATION

You can't prevent stimulation. Like the door-to-door salesman, it'll show up uninvited and unannounced. You can, though, decide *not* to entertain it. That's your management goal, and it's reachable. In Day 19's material, we'll look at some practical ways of doing this; but for now, this much should be settled:

1. It's no sin to be sexual. You were created that way.

2. It's no sin to be sexually tempted. How you respond to the temptation determines whether or not you've sinned.

3. When temptation begins (stimulation), your goal is to decide not to entertain the stimulation.

Can you choose to not give in to temptation? Without question. Let's close this section with two hopeful and astute observations the apostle Paul made about sin and its relation to you as a Player: "For sin shall not have dominion over you" (Romans 6:14). It will be present, in other words, but not all-powerful. It will be with you—enticing and distracting—but you aren't doomed to indulge in it.

Why? Because, as Paul confidently points out one book later: "God is faithful, who will not allow you to be tempted beyond what you are able, but with the temptation will also make the way of escape, that you may be able to bear it" (1 Corinthians 10:13).

Day 18

ACTION PLAN FOR UNDERSTANDING TEMPTATION

KEY VERSE

Therefore, in all things He [Jesus] had to be made like His brethren, that He might be a merciful and faithful High Priest in things pertaining to God, to make propitiation for the sins of the people. For in that He Himself has suffered, being tempted, He is able to aid those who are tempted.

—HEBREWS 2:17–18

PRINCIPLE

The better you know your system and what's going to be expected of it, the more capable you'll be as its manager. Your ability to be tempted and the options you have when tempted are two issues you especially have to understand. Temptation is guaranteed, but so is your God-given ability to resist it and a God-provided way of escape when temptations come.

ACTION

Write or type into your computer the answers to the following questions.

1. Temptations come either from within your own thoughts and desires, from Satan, or from others. Looking back over the past month, when was the last time you were stimulated just by

thoughts or desires that came purely from within you? How did you respond to them? How *should* you have responded?

2. Describe the last time you were directly tempted by another person. How did you respond? How *should* you have responded?

3. Describe the last time you felt Satan himself threw a temptation at you. How did you respond? How *should* you have responded?

4. What do you think Paul meant in Romans 6:14 when he said, "Sin shall not have dominion over you?" Be specific.

5. When was the last time you remember God providing for you a "way of escape" when you were tempted? Did you take it? Why or why not?

RATIONALE

By reviewing past times of temptations, you get a better idea what sort of triggers usually entice you and where (self, others, Satan) they tend to come from. It also gives you opportunity to review the kind of decisions you've made in the past, when tempted, and consider the type of decisions you want to make in the future.

PRAYER

Father, when I consider the thousands of times I'm tempted each day—or at least, what seem to be the thousands of times—I'm overwhelmed. Temptations fly at me so fast and often I can't imagine being able to respond in the right way. And I'd be less than honest if I didn't admit that, at times, I really don't want to respond in the right way. At times I've enjoyed lust as a boy enjoys a favorite toy, and to relinquish is a challenge.

Give me, then, an even deeper hatred for sin as I move into the training part of this process. Help me see more clearly what compromise has done to me, and refresh my zeal to say no to it.

You promised a way of escape when temptations come. Thank You for being so gracious and patient with me as I try, in my own faltering way, to find it. I ask this in Jesus's name. Amen.

GAME STATUS UPON COMPLETION OF SECTION THREE

By the end of Section Three (Understanding), you should have done the following: (Check off each item you've completed.)

_____ Identified the external triggers (triggers in the physical environment) that most commonly arouse you.

_____ Reduced, as much as possible, external triggers in your home, car, or place of business by reviewing your entertainment and information materials (TV shows, movies, magazines, and so on).

_____ Carefully read Ephesians 6:12–17 regarding spiritual warfare.

_____ Determined if there is someone with whom you need to discuss a deep and long-term wound, determined how that wound has been affecting you, and if applicable, contacted this individual to consider a frank discussion.

_____ Considered, in your own words, what Paul meant when he wrote, "Sin shall not have dominion over you" and what he meant when he promised that God would provide a "way of escape."

If you've left any of these action items undone, go back and complete them before continuing to Section Four.

SECTION FOUR

R

Day 19 Temptation-Resistance
Techniques

*We develop tools to use when faced with
temptation and practice resistance on a
daily basis.*

O

Day 20 Action Plan for
Resisting Temptation

Day 21 Entitlement

*We examine the "entitled" mind-set and the
pride and self-will that go along with it, and
we learn to put our attitude back under God's
governing.*

TRAINING

Day 22 Action Plan for Overcoming
Entitlement

E

Day 23 Boundaries

*We examine the problem of passivity and learn
to develop boundaries and, when necessary,
confront others.*

Day 24 Action Plan for Developing Boundaries

DAY 19

TEMPTATION-RESISTANCE TECHNIQUES

We are involved in a battle, and that means we must be constantly alert for new strategies both in defense and offense.

—ERWIN LUTZER, *LIVING WITH YOUR PASSIONS*

You wanna talk stupid? *Really* stupid? Pumping iron in a gym full of professional bodybuilders—now, that's stupid.

But there I was, struggling with a ninety-pound barbell on my shoulders next to a former Mr. America who was doing the same move with three times the weight. I'd joined this gym because I'd been told, "If you want to train hard, train with the best." Good advice, but the guy who gave it to me forgot to add: ". . . and when you train with the best, you'll feel like the worst."

And the wimpiest. I creaked out a few reps, checking my form in the mirror, when I noticed my reflection next to the gorilla working out beside me. Both of us were shirtless; one of us shouldn't have been. I sighed, plunked down my barbell, covered up, and muttered, "Idiot!"

"What's that?" Mr. America asked with a glare, and my wimpy life flashed in front of me.

"No, no—me. *Me*, I'm the idiot," I stammered. "Just talking to myself. Sorry."

"You need a wider grip," he answered.

"Huh?"

He put his weights down and turned toward me. "Your grip's

too narrow for a shoulder press. That's why you're not getting a pump in your delts." And within five minutes he corrected my form, recommended other shoulder exercises, and threw in a few diet tips.

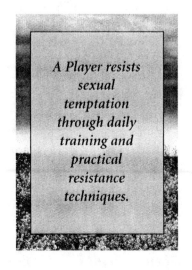

Pretty helpful for a gorilla. So helpful, in fact, I took advantage of his good nature by asking one last question: "So which is better—free weight resistance or machine resistance?"

"Flake resistance."

"Flake *what?*"

"Flake resistance," he repeated. "That's the main thing. Every time your body wants to chomp on the wrong food or skip a work-out or drink too much, you pull out any tool you can to resist flaking out. That's flake resistance. Build *that* up, and you can do anything."

A Player resists sexual temptation through daily training and practical resistance techniques.

He's been retired twenty-some years, but that guy is, and always will be, my champion.

A Player Lives a Life of Resistance

This section of the process—training—is about resisting the old familiar urges: the urge to compromise, indulge, give up, and in general, flake. To *flake* is to give in to desires that are in conflict with your goals. And any serious Player knows those desires will come often, and at times, they'll come strong.

Your goal, then, is to develop *temptation-resistance techniques.* Those are the tools you use to adopt new responses to old stimuli. For the next six days, we'll adopt and develop these tools, and they'll equip you to respond differently to sexual and relational triggers.

To understand the concept of resistance techniques, let's compare your situation to that of a guy who's just had a heart attack.

Suppose he's about fifty-five years old and very sedentary. Worse still, he eats all the wrong foods, and plenty of them. Then there's his smoking habit—two packs daily, let's say—and his penchant for lying around the house all day watching television.

He's incorporated some pretty bad patterns, but try telling *him* that! Over the years, you see, he's gotten comfortable with his compromise. Although he knows his lifestyle is bad, he rationalizes that it's not all *that* bad.

Until he has a crisis of truth. The heart attack hits him unexpectedly, and the experience is terrifying, providing a much-needed wake-up call. Just home from the hospital and frightened into action, he repents.

Out go the junk food and the cigarettes. He commits to a nutritious diet, moderate exercise, and healthy living, realizing his compromise nearly cost him everything. He turns, in other words, *from* a destructive lifestyle and *toward* a responsible one.

He also establishes allies. He meets with a physical trainer, joins a support group for overeaters and one for recovering smokers, and gets some accountability and encouragement. And, of course, he gets a better understanding of his circulatory system by studying books on the heart and its proper maintenance.

He's gone through repentance, order, and understanding—so far, so good. But he'll still need to train, because no matter how sincerely he wants to stay away from junk food and nicotine, the urge to use both will, at some point, return. And like Ulysses' sirens, those urges sing one sweet song! He's spent years indulging them; now he'll spend years resisting them. And resistance won't be a cakewalk, so let's hope he develops the best tools possible, because his very life is at stake.

As is yours. You've had your crisis of truth, leading you to turn from and toward. You've established order and allies, and you've developed a better understanding of your system—what it needs, how it works, what to avoid. So far, so good. Now you'll incorporate resistance techniques as well, because the urge to compromise will come, and with it comes the possibility of dismantling all the good work you've done so far.

That's a possibility you're not going to entertain, so let's train.

A COOPERATIVE EFFORT

Training is a cooperative effort between God and man. We see this principle throughout the Bible, when God calls a man to a purpose and says, in essence, "Here's the goal. This is what My part is in achieving it; here's your part." Of course, we're not equals in our partnership with God, and He doesn't *need* us to fulfill His purposes. But in His wisdom, He's chosen to include us in them. And so, when fulfilling them, we trust Him to do what we cannot do, and He entrusts us to do what we can.

Any evangelist will tell you that. Listen to Billy Graham, Greg Laurie, or Franklin Graham, and you'll hear words that have been carefully thought out. These men have been entrusted by God to prepare the most important message their listeners will ever hear, so you better believe they do their homework. They labor over each point, scour current events for sermon illustrations, and do their utmost to prepare and even polish their presentations. Entrusted by God, they do what they can.

Then, having delivered their message, they trust God to do what they *cannot*. They cannot save anyone; they cannot convict; they cannot force anyone to come forward. That is God's work alone, and it constitutes His part of the cooperative effort between God and evangelist.

Your training is similar. God alone can transform your heart; He alone can save and sanctify you. Yet you're required to do your part in the sanctification process, and that's where training—an act of human effort—comes in.

When a Christian man routinely sins, he's got two general problems: a hardened conscience and a lack of impulse control. He's hardened his conscience by ignoring it over the years, and his impulse control is weak or, in some cases, virtually nonexistent.

Conscience is softened when God allows a crisis that awakens the heart and redirects the man. His daily disciplines—prayer, Bible study, recommitment, and motive review—also affect his conscience daily, softening his heart toward God and making him all the more sensitive to His Spirit.

But there's still the problem of impulse control. That's the muscle we exercise when we say no to whatever is appealing but, at the same time, destructive or counterproductive. It's a mental and emotional muscle, and everybody has one. It's mental, because impulse control is an act of the *will*. (For example, we *will* to say no when something looks good but doesn't fit our plans or our ethics.)

It's an emotional muscle, too, because when we feel like something would be pleasurable and nice, yet we know it's counterproductive, we "flex" emotionally by denying ourselves the thing our feelings crave.

Some men make the mistake of waiting for God to give them impulse control when, in fact, He already has. They're just not using it. It's like your other muscles. When people see a well-developed bodybuilder, they say, "Wow! He's got muscles!"

Sure, but so do you. We all do. The difference between most of us and the bodybuilder is that he's chosen to exercise his muscles intensely and regularly. So it is with impulse control. You already have it, but like an underused muscle, it may be weak.

We're going to change that, starting today.

Training Goal: Keeping Temptation Cycles in Check

Remember the cycle we discussed two days ago? When you're tempted, it begins with stimulation, which you may or may not "let in." If you let it in, you begin entertaining it, which is a slippery slope, often leading to indulgence. It's a pattern similar to the one James described in his epistle when he referred to temptation, lust, and consequence (James 1:14–15—see below).

SIMULATION	ENTERTAINMENT	INDULGENCE
You're aroused and decide whether or not to entertain the arousal.	You entertain the arousal with a second look, a fantasy, or a flirtation.	You relapse by acting on the stimulation.
"Each one is tempted when he is drawn away by his own desires and enticed . . ." (v. 14)	"Then, when desire has conceived, it gives birth to sin . . ." (v. 15)	". . . and sin, when it is full-grown, brings forth death." (v. 15)

You're not going to avoid stimulation, the first part of this cycle. It's everywhere, so you'll be stimulated, not necessarily because you choose to be but because it's a part of life. Just consider the triggers in the environment, in the spiritual realm, and in your internal world that stimulate you in different ways:

PHYSICAL ENVIRONMENT	SPIRITUAL REALM (SATANIC DEVICES)	INTERNAL WORLD
• attractive people	• seduction	• fantasies
• sexy images	• accusations	• memories
• flirtatious people	• discord	• dreams
• suggestive song lyrics	• condemnation	• attractions
• erotic media messages	• deceit	• old wounds
		• negative moods

These physical, spiritual, and psychological elements create either sexual stimulation or emotional discomfort, both of which make sexual sin look like an attractive "medication." In other words, there's a lot of stimulation waiting out there for you.

So if you try to avoid being stimulated, you'll be frustrated. Temptation happens, and, remember, it's no sin to be tempted. Instead, your goal is to resist letting the stimulation go into the entertainment phase. And that's where resistance training comes in.

I'm going to propose two simple temptation-resistance techniques you can incorporate and use daily. It will take practice, moderate effort, and consistent application—that's your part of the cooperative effort. So let's get to it.

BUT FIRST, SUIT UP!

You'd never, I hope, play ice hockey without the proper gear: padding, mask, helmet, and shin guards. Nor would you play football or baseball, for that matter, without some protection. Suiting up, so you can handle the rigors of the game, is basic to any sport.

How much more, then, should you be suited up—armor in place—before meeting the daily challenges of the world, the flesh, and the devil? Paul tells us "the whole armor of God" is standard attire for any man wanting to "withstand in the evil day, and having done all, to stand" (Ephesians 6:13).

So, as the ad says, don't leave home without it.

In practical terms, that means *never* be so stupid as to begin your day without prayer. (Playing hockey in a pair of Speedos would be smarter, believe me.) It's the arena you're going into, not the spa, so be prepared.

Your daily discipline includes prayer and Scripture reading because they're essential, and part of your prayer life includes taking on your armor:

"Stand therefore, having girded your waist with truth" (Ephesians 6:14). The truth you take in from your Scripture reading covers your loins, where so many vital organs are. Truth keeps you from falling for the many lies you're likely to encounter on any given day.

"Put on the breastplate of righteousness" (v. 14). In prayer you're built up spiritually, strengthening your faith in the righteousness of Christ that's been imparted to you. To play well, you need a regular reminder that it's in His righteousness alone you can take a bold stand.

"Shod your feet with the preparation of the gospel of peace" (v. 15). Both your prayer time and Scripture reading clarify in your mind the difference between the saved and the unsaved. This, in turn, keeps you "gospel aware"—that is, aware that there's a heaven and a hell, and that everyone you encounter is bound for one or

the other. No one who stays aware of this can be unaffected, in his speech and conduct, by that knowledge.

"[Take] the shield of faith with which you will be able to quench all the fiery darts of the wicked one" (v. 16). Faith comes by hearing, Paul said, and hearing by the Word of God. By exposing yourself to it daily, your faith grows and your protective shield is strengthened. Your enemy's attacks, relentless as they are, can't harm you.

"And take the helmet of salvation, and the sword of the Spirit, which is the word of God" (v. 17). Knowing your position in Christ, being reminded of it daily, and getting into the habit of speaking the Word regularly—all three cover your thought life and arm you with what you need to deal with the aggressions of the arena and your opponent.

DISTRACTION: RESISTING VISUAL TRIGGERS

Then, having suited up, you play. To get a sense of the playing field, let's look at a typical man's routine.

He drives to work, applies himself on the job, has lunch, leaves the office, and stops at the gym for a workout. Then maybe he goes to a restaurant for dinner, drives home again, and plops down in front of the television.

And in the midst of all this routine activity, he's bombarded with "visuals."

There's the sexy billboard he passes on the way to work, then the voluptuous girl he sees in the parking lot. He enters the office and bumps into the aggressive co-worker who dresses to kill and loves to flirt. He breaks for lunch, only to find someone brought the *Sports Illustrated* swimsuit issue into the lunchroom, thanks a lot. Worse still is the porn magazine someone left in the men's room.

After work, he finds the women at the gym are in skin-tight workout attire. At dinner, the waitress wears a low-cut uniform, and on the way home he passes the same billboard he wishes he'd avoided this morning. Finally, when he gets home and clicks the remote, the ads on television parade one beautiful body after another. And through all this, he's supposed to keep his mind pure.

The good news? Tomorrow it will start again.

That's the arena, the sexually idolatrous environment where The Game is played. All day long you're bombarded with visuals, stimulating you and inviting you to "entertain" them by looking, lusting, or worse. The distraction technique can help you resist. It's a simple three-part exercise: shift, breathe, recite.

First, you *shift*. Men are visual creatures, and there's nothing wrong with that. We are constantly assessing (or "checking out") our surroundings. So when we walk into a room, we assess the size of the room, the number of people inside, and so forth.

When you assess the environment, you'll sometimes spot what I call a "candidate." That's someone who's your *type*. She attracts you, and you're drawn by the desire to go on looking at her, enjoying both her beauty and the high that comes from lusting after her. (Or her image, if it's a magazine cover or picture of some sort that's triggering you.)

You may have noticed that when you spot a candidate, it's as though an electric current goes from you to her. It happens quickly, much as it did to King David that notorious night on the rooftop. If you don't disconnect quickly, you'll get pulled in deeper, either into an erotic fantasy or, worse still, a sexual encounter. At that moment you need something that will help you disconnect ASAP.

So you shift visual gears, by refocusing your eyes immediately to anything safe (an object or a person you're not at all attracted to). When you do that, you're changing channels mentally (or shifting gears, if you prefer).

Jesus alluded to this, by the way, when He taught about the power of the eye: "The lamp of the body is the eye. Therefore, when your eye is good, your whole body also is full of light. But when your eye is bad, your body also is full of darkness" (Luke 11:34).

What you focus on has more impact than you've probably realized. So when you refocus, you shift to something safe.

Then you *breathe*, deeply and quietly. The value of deep breathing is that, in tough situations, it helps you regain control. If you're very angry and ready to pop someone, for example, a few deep breaths can calm you down. Or when you're panicking, it's amazing what deep breathing does to stabilize you. Or, in this case, to cool you down and prevent stimulation from going any further.

Then, as you breathe, you *recite*.

Try it now as you read this. Put down the book, then look at an object, breathe deeply, then recite any of the following five scriptures:

> I have made a covenant with my eyes;
>   why then should I look upon a young woman? (Job 31:1)

> I have made a covenant in perfect peace,
>   Whose mind is stayed on You. (Isaiah 26:3)

> Present your bodies a living sacrifice, holy, acceptable to God. (Romans 12:1)

> When desire has conceived, it gives birth to sin. (James 1:15)

> I must be about My Father's business. (Luke 2:49)

That last verse works awfully well for me!

Simple enough? It's meant to be. The distraction technique works for visual triggers, because it gives you a window in which you can cool down, mentally and physically, when someone (or something) stimulates you. And during that cool-down period, you give yourself enough control to decide *not* to entertain the stimulation. It looks pretty much like this:

1. You assess your surroundings.
2. You spot someone or something that triggers a stimulation.
3. You risk losing control as you're stimulated.
4. You shift your eyes to any "safe" (nonarousing) object or person.
5. You breathe deeply, then recite one or more of the scriptures listed above.
6. You regain control.

Start practicing this technique the next time anything in the environment stimulates you. (You'll do so in your action plan tomorrow.) I use it often, with good results.

When I'm driving, for example, and I pass something or someone who triggers me, I can shift my visual gears to the road or to the car in front of me, take a few deep breaths, recite, and regain control. Or in a crowded room, if someone looks like a "candidate," I'm pretty much able to do this exercise even when I'm conversing with someone. The more you practice, the more easily and automatically it comes.

At first it can be clumsy. I've taught this technique at seminars and then gone out for dinner with the men who attended. It's been hilarious, I'll admit, watching the guys do their "homework" as the waitress leans forward to take their orders and they say, "I'll have the steak . . . (*'I have made a covenant . . .'*) medium well . . . (*'Present your bodies a living sacrifice . . .'*)" all the while staring hard at their menus and avoiding eye contact.

Still, the more you use it, the more naturally and gracefully it comes to you. And insignificant as this little exercise seems, keep this in mind: it's often the second look that dismantles a man's life.

One quick glance away from Bathsheba might have spared David a catastrophe. A brief distraction might have given Samson a chance to use his head. And who knows what agony might have been avoided if a former president had shifted his gaze from a White House intern?

So keep this technique handy. It can change your legacy.

REALITY CHECK

The distraction technique is great for visuals, which tend to be brief and fleeting. But there are other times temptation seems relentless, and it's not even clear why it's coming on so strong.

There can be so many reasons for this. Physical reasons, maybe, such as seminal fluid that has built up if you haven't had an orgasm for some time. Or emotional reasons—loneliness, frustration, resentment—or spiritual elements, maybe? Who knows. An ongoing desire for a sexual release gets brought on by any number of things, but what matters is, it's *ongoing!*

During those times of long, drawn-out temptations, when the desire to relapse seems unbearable, I find the reality check a very helpful resistance tool.

When you use the reality check, you verbalize your name, the name of the people closest to you, and your primary responsibilities. You say each of these out loud, concentrating on what you're saying. And in doing so, you throw some pretty cold water on your sexual temptation.

THE REALITY CHECK DIFFUSES COMPARTMENTALIZATION

When you "act out"—use porn, commit adultery, fornicate—you have to mentally block out the most important aspects of your life. If you don't, you'll have a difficult time trying to enjoy the sin! It's tough, you know, to masturbate to Internet pornography while thinking about God or your wife and children.

I'll bet you were a little repulsed by my even saying that. See? The two worlds of sexual sin and your life's priorities (God, family, calling) can't coexist, so one has to be blocked out when you're engaging the other.

No wonder so many men use an alias when they "act out." If they go to a bar or hire a prostitute or get into a sex-oriented chat room, they seldom use their real name. And while there may be practical reasons for this (like fear of exposure), I believe there are emotional reasons too. It's easier for a man to adopt another name when he sins, because that makes it easier for him not to face the fact that it's really *he* who's sinning.

And that's the power of the reality check. By keeping in your mind's forefront the people who matter most, you'll find it harder to indulge in something that could destroy them.

I use this one frequently when I travel, since hotels can be lonely places, and I'm easily depressed when I've been away from my family for more than a day. So when the temptation to masturbate or mentally compromise hits, I find it very helpful to say out loud: "My name is Joe Dallas. My wife's name is Renee; my sons are Jody and Jeremy. I'm a pastoral counselor, and I run a ministry called Genesis Counseling."

Just saying this out loud diffuses temptation, because the people I love and the things that matter to me can't coexist, even in my mind, with sexual sin.

When you use the reality check, then, you say three things out loud:

1. Your name

2. The names of the people most important to you

3. Your life responsibilities (job, ministry, calling)

You'll try this technique, too, during your action plan tomorrow. Keep it handy when you need to resist long-term, ongoing temptation. As a simple mental exercise, it's surprisingly effective.

In your prayer closet, you prepare for the arena. Then, during the average day, you enter and play The Game, and much of your success or failure is determined by your "flake resistance," as my bodybuilding friend put it so nicely. Let's close by thinking about how meaningful this business of training can be.

THE PURPOSE OF TRAINING

Paul had some interesting advice about the proper use of our bodies: "And do not present your members [body parts] as instruments of unrighteousness to sin, but present yourselves to God as being alive from the dead, and your members as instruments of righteousness to God" (Romans 6:13).

The resistance of sin is an act of worship. When you resist, you refuse to yield your body parts to an activity that you might, in fact, take some real pleasure in. But rather than conform your body to unrighteousness, you conform it to Him. And so it becomes a worship instrument.

I play the piano, and there are few things I've loved as much as playing in church, using the keyboard as an instrument of praise. I used to do it full-time, when I was very young, and the experience was awesome.

But nowadays I'm pretty rusty on the ivories. No time for practice—I hardly ever play anymore. But that's OK, because I've got another praise instrument: my body. Every time I say no to lust, every time I tear my eyes away from the sexy magazine cover, every time I refuse to entertain the dirty thought that just passed through my unruly brain, it's an act of worship. It's my own unique, meaningful hymn:

> *In this moment of resistance, I love You.*
> *Here's how I love You—by not indulging.*
> *My body is Yours, so I say no to whatever You hate.*
> *And by saying no to it, I'm saying a loving, wholehearted yes to You.*
> *Receive my worship.*

He does, and He will. So don't resist sexual sin just for the sake of purity, important as that is. Make training an act of worship, and see for yourself how deep and meaningful daily love through resistance can really be.

DAY 20

ACTION PLAN FOR RESISTING TEMPTATION

KEY VERSE

Therefore we also, since we are surrounded by so great a cloud of witnesses, let us lay aside every weight, and the sin which so easily ensnares us, and let us run with endurance the race that is set before us.

—HEBREWS 12:1

PRINCIPLE

Training means adopting a lifestyle of resisting temptation and yielding your body to God. You have the specific goal of recognizing sexual temptation when it comes and keeping it from going beyond the stimulation phase. To do so, you adopt a "second language" of resistance, made up of different techniques and principles. Today you're going to begin practicing a few.

ACTION

1. Practice the distraction technique (refocus, breathe, count) by doing the following:

   a. Sit in a chair and pick out an object in the room (a piece of furniture, a book, a chair). Make that your "candidate" (potential object of lust).

   b. Pick out another object similar to the first, and make it your "safety."

   c. Look briefly at your "candidate" and immediately refocus to your "safety." Breathe in and out through your nose and recite one of the five verses listed on page 142. Be sure you don't just rattle them off—think about the words.

   d. Repeat steps a, b, and c four more times.

2. Practice the reality check technique by doing the following:

   a. Sit in a chair, take three deep breaths, and relax, clearing your mind.

   b. Say the following out loud: your name, the names of your wife and children or three of the people you're closest to, and the responsibilities you have that would be affected negatively if you sexually sinned.

   c. Repeat steps a and b four more times.

3. Begin practicing these techniques when you're stimulated, and discuss with your accountability partner and group how they're impacting you.

RATIONALE

Indulging in lust has been your primary language for years. In order to learn the secondary language of resistance, you need to practice it daily and immerse yourself both in it and in the company of others who speak it as well.

PRAYER

Father, I enter into training knowing there's much I cannot do and much I have to do! I can't make my own heart pure, nor can I make myself hate sin as I know You'd have me hate it. I can't keep temptations from coming my way, and I can't erase all the sexual images and memories I've created for myself. I'm repentant but polluted by my own wrong decisions. So I ask You to do what I cannot do—purify me.

What I can do, I will, by Your grace. Give me the awareness to spot temptation when it comes and the strength to resist by not allowing myself to entertain it. Give me patience, too, with myself, and give my loved ones patience with me as I sometimes clumsily go about my training.

Please accept my resistance of sin as an offering—a personal act of worship unto You. I ask this in Jesus's name. Amen.

DAY 21

ENTITLEMENT

*God sends no one away empty except those who
are full of themselves.*

—D. L. MOODY

When I repented in January 1984, I nearly drowned in grief over my failures. I was forced to look not just at my wrongdoing, but at its effects as well. And that meant asking myself questions I'd avoided for six years.

I wondered, for example, how God must have felt when I walked into that adult bookstore and said, in essence, "*This* matters more to me than *You*, so I choose *this*." That was a road I'd never let my thoughts go down before.

And what about my old friends, the people I'd known and ministered to? How had *they* felt when they heard I was backslidden? How disappointed had they been; how angry were they with me? It was impossible to believe I hadn't stumbled some of them, but how many? And had my open, wild rebellion encouraged any of them to do as I'd done?

That was too much. I was forgiven, yes, but now I was also incredibly ashamed as I looked at the wasteland my behavior had caused. And worst of all, the more I thought about the wrong I'd done, the clearer it became that I was powerless to undo it.

I started praying daily for forgiveness, conjuring up and confessing every sin I could remember. And while I ransacked my memory to be sure there weren't any unconfessed sins slipping through the cracks, I felt God's still, small voice tugging at me.

Now, I'm not big on "God told me." There are very few times in my life I feel He has spoken directly to me, but this was one of them.

"You *still* don't get it." He seemed to be saying it over and over.

"Get what?" I wondered out loud. Was I missing something— some wrong I hadn't remembered or, worse yet, wasn't willing to remember?

"Your real sin. You still don't get it."

My real *sin?* "Show me," I whispered. "Please show me."

"Idol worship. Other gods, one in particular. You made a god of Joe Dallas. Everything else you did sprang from that, and where did your god get you? Renounce him and come back to Me."

And I've been renouncing that false god—sometimes effectively, sometimes poorly—ever since.

REJECTING DIVINE AUTHORITY

The sin of entitlement is the rejection of God's authority. It was Lucifer's original sin when he plotted to become like God, usurping His position (Isaiah 14:12–15). It was Adam's sin when he willingly disobeyed (Genesis 3:6), and it's humanity's great sin described in Romans 1 when, according to Paul, "although they knew God, they did not glorify Him as God, nor were thankful, but became futile in their thoughts, and their foolish hearts were darkened" (v. 21).

The creation knows it has a Creator but rejects Him when His authority becomes inconvenient. That's entitlement—a mind-set that's exposed by our behavior when we act as though we answer to no one but ourselves. And I feel it's one of the most common, most pervasive problems among Christian men who allow themselves to sexually sin.

To play well, you need an athlete's *mind* as well as his *habits.* So through repentance, God calls you to turn from sinful behavior. Then, in the first part of training, He calls you to resist sinful temptations. Now, in this second part of training, He calls you to reject a way of thinking that may have created the behavior. So today we'll explore the entitled mind-set, looking at its origins, its ongoing effects, and ways we can overcome it.

"Mine!"

If you've raised children, you are very familiar with the four-letter word they learn at about age two and repeat over and over: "Mine, mine, *mine!*"

Pick up a toy the kid discarded hours ago, and your hand gets slapped: "Mine!" Try removing the plate he hasn't touched at dinner, and suddenly "Mine!" gets screamed at you full throttle. Everything, it seems, has become "Mine!" as your little darling's narcissism kicks into gear. It's exasperating but understandable. Part of the child's development relies on his coming to terms with the fact that the world is *not* entirely himself, nor is it his. And who faces up to that without a little kicking and screaming?

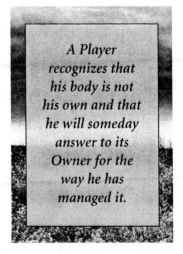

A Player recognizes that his body is not his own and that he will someday answer to its Owner for the way he has managed it.

Don't get too smug, my friend. You did it, too, I'm sure, putting your parents through the same nonsense. And nowhere, I'll wager, did the "Mine!" concept take root as strongly as it did when you discovered your genitals.

Now that, you thought, *is* really *mine!* You played with it, enjoyed it, and took ownership of it. That, too, is understandable; but think of the mind-set that goes along with early self-pleasuring: *This is mine, to enjoy and entertain myself with however I choose.* That mind-set plays into later sexual experiments, which tend to be wildly selfish. "Mine!" says the junior high stud, pushing his girlfriend past her limits, taking what he can and caring little about the impact it has on her. "Mine!" says the high school Romeo, conquering girl after girl, recounting each conquest with endless locker-room bragging. "Sex is for me; it's mine, and nothing else matters."

For some men, "Mine!" becomes a lifelong religion they practice faithfully. Others, though, encounter something more substantial. They hear the gospel of Jesus Christ, and they respond. In doing so, they agree to a covenant that requires a whole new way of thinking: "Do you not know that your body is a temple of the Holy Spirit who is in you, whom you have from God, and you are not your own? For you were bought at a price; therefore glorify God in your body and in your spirit, which are God's" (1 Corinthians 6:19–20).

Now it's no longer "Mine!" It's "Thine." You made that agreement when you were born again, and I think you meant it. I think you understood you were no longer your own, that your body now belonged to God, and that you'd willingly entered into a contract with specific, reasonable terms.

I wonder, though, if you realized those terms applied to your genitals. After all, when we refer to our body as the Spirit's temple, it seems almost blasphemous to suggest the temple includes our private parts. We tend to separate them from that concept, because what on earth would He want with *that*? I'm inclined to think God wants my head, shoulders, arms, mouth—the respectable parts. He couldn't be interested in anything below the waist, so I'm prone to think *that* area can't glorify Him. And if it can't, it's not under His jurisdiction and still belongs, therefore, to me.

"Mine!" At least something is still mine. Can you see how easy it becomes, then, to indulge myself sexually, privately, all the while telling myself that I *do* glorify God with my body? (At least, I'm glorifying God with the parts of my body that matter to Him.)

That's entitled thinking. At some point, as part of your sanctification, God will put His finger on it and reclaim ownership.

NOTICE FROM THE LANDLORD

My wife and I own rental property, which means, of course, setting up contracts and terms with people who want to rent from us.

Most of our tenants have been great, but every so often, someone gets confused as to who owns the property and who rents it.

We try to be reasonable. If someone wants to paint the interior, OK. Plant some of their own flowers? No problem. But there are some definite "thou shalt nots." No knocking down walls, no painting the exterior, no sneaking in additional tenants who aren't on the rental agreement. And if someone decides not to comply, I have to play the heavy.

At times like that, I remind the renter of the basics: he didn't have to rent from me; I didn't put a gun to his head and say, "Move in." He agreed to certain terms; if he didn't want to comply with them, he shouldn't have agreed to them. And if he really wants his own place, he should buy, not rent.

I hardly ever have to give that speech. It's reserved only for people who forget the original terms.

Now, your body is God's temple, not yours. You live in it, certainly, and you're given a good deal of leeway. I doubt God gets too heavy-handed about what color tie you should wear, or whether or not you should put cream in your coffee. Many of the choices you make regarding your body are left to your discretion.

But some aren't, and there are some definite "thou shalt nots." Sexual acting out violates your agreement; and if you decide not to comply, you'll eventually hear from the Landlord.

He'll knock on the door, invite Himself in, and remind you of the basics. You didn't have to enter into the salvation covenant with Him; He didn't put a gun to your head and say, "Receive Me." You agreed to His terms. If you didn't want to comply with them, you shouldn't have agreed to them. And if you really want your own place—well, sorry. You gave up the title.

But maybe you forgot that. Maybe, while incorporating and protecting a sexual sin, you told yourself you were essentially obedient—well, obedient enough, anyway, in so many other areas. ("Look how much I tithe weekly and how much volunteer work I do for the church!") This one area, you decided, didn't really count. So every time you compromised, you strengthened the mind-set that says, "Mine!"

That's because every act of entitlement—that is, every self-willed, self-justified rebellion (as in, "I know this is wrong, but I'll do it anyway!") fuels the entitled mind-set. It's an ugly dynamic. When you transgress, you reinforce the "Mine!" way of thinking. That, in turn, makes it easier to transgress the next time you're tempted. And each future transgression strengthens, yet again, the "Mine!" mentality, which makes future transgression easier . . . you get the picture.

So now that you've repented and are well into your training, you've got to deal with "Mine!"—that insidious, creepy, entitled thinking that tells you when you're tired or moody: "Hey, I deserve a break. I've been good. No porn; no hookers. So if I kick back and enjoy a little masturbation fantasy, no big deal. I'm a guy, after all, and it's the reward I deserve for staying sober for so long. I'm a Christian, sure, but a man's gotta be entitled to *something!*"

Sounds like a small vice, hardly worth mentioning. Yet it's those seemingly small compromises that bring a man crashing down. C. S. Lewis nailed this concept when he wrote: "He cannot bless us unless He has us. When we try to keep within us an area that is our own, we try to keep an area of death. Therefore, in love, He claims all. There's no bargaining with Him."[13]

Israel learned this when they finally entered the Promised Land. After their wanderings, Joshua brought them over the Jordan River while God stilled the waters, giving them safe entry and securing both their new home and their new leader. Their first conquest was to be Jericho, and after their triumphal entry, the Israelites must have been pumped and ready for battle.

But then God gave Joshua a curious command: "Make flint knives for yourself, and circumcise the sons of Israel" (Joshua 5:2).

Can you imagine informing the men (just before a battle, no less) that God had a surprise for them? It's easy to imagine someone from the troops stepping forward, wide-eyed and stammering, "Excuse me, sir, but we were just wondering—respectfully, of course—you want to *what?* And *why?*"

Why, indeed? Circumcision before a battle doesn't sound too bright. There'd have to be a recovery period with bleeding, weakness, and undue delays. What's the point?

Joshua's record makes it clear: "And this is the reason why Joshua circumcised them: All the people who came out of Egypt who were males, all the men of war, had died in the wilderness on the way, after they had come out of Egypt. For all the people who came out had been circumcised, but all the people born in the wilderness, on the way as they came out of Egypt, had not been circumcised" (vv. 4–5).

These people belonged to God. He'd just miraculously moved on their behalf, in fact. Yet there was something missing in their relationship to Him. They were uncircumcised, even as they followed Him. And circumcision, you'll remember, was a covenant sign of their separation to Him (Genesis 17:10–13).

Their separation! They carried His name, but they weren't, in fact, playing the game. They remained, in a seemingly small but in fact crucial way, separated *from* Him, not *toward* Him. And He would no longer tolerate that compromise.

But why now? Why, just before such an important event as their battle with Jericho, did He suddenly decide to remedy the long-standing problem?

Even though it's not spelled out, it seems plain to me: if Israel didn't correct the problem of compromise in their most private area, they'd be unfit and unprepared for the battles they'd soon face. They took Jericho down, as you know. But I can't imagine them doing so if they'd remained uncircumcised and un-separated. And the effects of Joshua's actions were immediate: "Then the LORD said to Joshua, 'This day I have rolled away the reproach of Egypt from you'" (v. 9).

Entitlement, in mind-set or action, brings its own reproach. Because when you're not truly separated to Him, you're unfit and unprepared for the battles you'll face.

If we learned anything from the attacks of September 11, 2001, it's that we haven't a clue what challenges we'll be called to rise to. Before that day's horror, we never imagined an event like that on our own shores. But we woke up, I hope, to the fact that we have enemies more lethal than we figured, and our future safety and comfort could never again be taken for granted.

So are you naive enough to think you'll not face another "unthinkable" challenge? Maybe not a terrorist attack, but it will be something more than what you thought you'd have to deal with— something you'll need to be strong enough, inwardly and outwardly, to face.

Your own Jericho. Are you ready?

Not if you still say from your heart, "Mine!" That's why God puts His finger on entitlement and says, "This, too, has to go."

A Player's Life, a Servant's Mind

How do you know if you've got an entitlement problem? You might ask yourself a few questions:

1. Do the people closest to you ever say that your words and attitude suggest an unusual amount of selfishness?
2. Even though you're resisting temptation, do you resent having to do it? Do you feel as though God unfairly took away your toys when He called you to repent?
3. Do you still envy other men who let themselves indulge in the things you've rejected?
4. Do you expect applause from friends and loved ones for staying sober, then pout (privately, of course) when you don't get it?
5. Do you demand that your wife "get over" the hurt you've caused her, and do you minimize that hurt by insisting she's making too much of it?
6. Do you think the rules others live by don't, or at least shouldn't, apply to you?

Answering yes to three or more of these questions indicates a problem. That means your way of thinking, not just your behavior, needs retraining. And retraining comes by changing your thoughts through your actions, and your actions through your thoughts.

I hope you're striving for greatness, so let's remember the advice Jesus gave anyone wanting to be great: "Whoever desires to become great among you, let him be your servant"(Matthew 20:26).

A great Player is a servant, and an eager one at that—one who seeks to serve all by putting their needs before his own. And that, we might as well admit, isn't our natural tendency.

We've spent much of our lives indulging ourselves. So much, in fact, that you could say indulgence has been our primary language. Your primary language is the one you grew up speaking, which now comes fluently and automatically to you. And no matter what other languages you learn, *that's* the one you're likely to resort to.

You can certainly learn a second language, though. It's the new language you adopt, and the more you practice it, the more fluently it comes. Immerse yourself in it, by speaking it and surrounding yourself with others who do the same, and it will come more quickly to you. And each time you speak it, you'll reinforce it.

Indulgence ("Mine!") has been your primary language. Now you're adopting a second language: servanthood. So every time you resist putting your needs above another person's, you're speaking your second language. The more you practice it, the more fluently it comes, and the more each act of service affects the entitled way of thinking.

Start by examining your closest relationships. Renew your commitment, daily, to finding ways to serve your friends and loved ones. Every act of service, especially every act that requires you to put your wants aside for the good of another, chips away at the "Mine!" mentality. And thus a champion's mind-set develops.

While you're letting your actions affect your mind-set, you should also train your mind-set to affect your behavior. You can do that by meditating on three points:

1. The standards God gave us

2. Our history of violating them

3. The madness that results

When you meditate on something, you think it through carefully, lingering over it while letting it sink in. Let's do that with our history, especially the ugly parts, because there's a lesson in there I want you to absorb.

Think first of God's standards: monogamy, honesty, sobriety, self-control, faithfulness. They're pretty clear, and He made no bones about their importance. Both testaments contain many references to them.

Then think long and hard about what happens when, in the past, you lived as though you belonged only to yourself. Isn't it true that when you take yourself out from under God's authority, you reject His standards as well? Your own history teaches you that, left to yourself, you'll step far and apart from biblical standards.

And where has that gotten you? When you took charge, entitled and independent, how successful was your life? What did your "ownership" do for your marriage, friendships, relation to God, peace of mind, and general well-being?

Look at it in another light: If you were the CEO of the corporation named You, would the board of directors keep you on?

No? Didn't think so, and that's the lesson I want you to absorb: "Mine" leads to madness!

How can we keep the entitled mind-set at bay? By simply remembering, as often as necessary, the shipwreck we made of our lives when we decided we, not He, should be appointed captain.

Admittedly, turning the wheel over to Him goes against our rebel grain. But it also cuts to the core of what we're trying to achieve as Players, believers, and disciples. The late Francis Schaeffer pointed this out when he wrote: "Here in the midst of life, there is to be a strong negative by choice. It is not, for example, a matter of waiting until we no longer have strong sexual desires, but rather that in the midst of the moving of life, surrounded by a world that grabs everything, we are to understand what Jesus means when He talks about denying ourselves that which is not rightfully ours."[14]

Denying ourselves, learning a second language, and remembering not only who we are but Whose we are. We do this not only because it's right to abandon, once and for all, the entitled mind-set, but because it's smart too.

That mind-set didn't work. We tried "Mine!" and it led to madness. God grant that we never forget it.

Day 22

ACTION PLAN FOR
OVERCOMING ENTITLEMENT

KEY VERSE

For you were bought at a price; therefore glorify God in your body and in your spirit, which are God's.

—1 CORINTHIANS 6:20

PRINCIPLE

Every deliberate sexual transgression you've committed has re-inforced in your mind the false notion that you're entitled to do with your body as you please. Entitlement, then, is a deeply ingrained error in thinking that has to be challenged and corrected if a Player wants to play from the heart.

ACTION

1. Read Romans 12:1–3. Notice how Paul begins this passage by saying, "I beseech you therefore, brethren, by the mercies of God." This means an awareness of God's mercies tends to soften our hearts toward Him. Write or type into your computer five specific and significant mercies God has shown you personally.

2. When you've forgotten His mercies in the past and yielded to your own desires while ignoring His, how do you think He has felt? Write specifically some of the feelings He's had when you've grieved Him.

3. Why do you think His feelings haven't mattered enough to you in the past to keep you from deliberate transgression?

4. How would you describe a man who lives his life as though he truly is a "living sacrifice"? How do you think that concept "living sacrifice" affects his speech and behavior?

5. How will being a "living sacrifice" change the way you personally act, speak, and think?

RATIONALE

Much of our reclaiming of created intent has to be done in the mind, which requires thinking through our past selfishness, indifference to God, and false notions about ourselves. Reflecting on these things helps prime our mental pump and prepare us mentally and emotionally to continue in serious training.

PRAYER

Father, the more I think about it, the more amazed I am by Your patience. I see more than ever how I've taken the body You gave me and treated it as though I was its creator, designer, and owner. I've chosen to ignore Your ownership when it's suited my purposes then clung to it when I've needed Your protection and grace. I've been a disciple when it's been convenient, which means I've been no disciple at all.

But more than ever, I hunger for a disciple's heart. Replace this rebel attitude, then, with the mind that was in Christ Jesus, who humbled Himself and became obedient even to the cross. In my own strength, I'll never attain that mind or follow that path. But through Your ongoing work in me, I look forward to doing what I, apart from You, could never accomplish. I ask this in Jesus's name. Amen.

Day 23

BOUNDARIES

*You will have to care enough to lovingly speak the truth,
even when you would rather gloss over a problem or ignore
an issue. Most people have no one in their life who loves
them enough to tell them the truth.*

—Rick Warren, *The Purpose Driven Life*

I'm bothered more by what I *should* have done than by anything I actually *have* done. One of my worst failures, in fact—a "should have done" tormenting me even now—came from my refusal to speak up and confront.

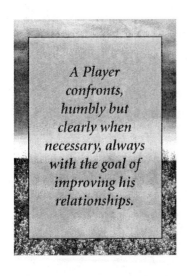

A Player confronts, humbly but clearly when necessary, always with the goal of improving his relationships.

Robert was an amazing man, gifted with insight, passion, and astonishing charisma. I first met him when he was leading a home Bible study, and though he wasn't yet twenty-one years old, he taught with an authority most forty-year-olds couldn't match. I was seventeen at the time, impressionable and eager, so when he eventually asked me to join his fledgling ministry, I jumped on it. Like all gifted leaders, he was a man you believed in and hitched up with.

Within three years, that home Bible study grew into a television and radio ministry, with services attended by a thousand-plus weekly and monthly rallies held throughout the state. The money flowed, our influence grew, and Robert changed. His style—once humble and funny—was now flamboyant and bossy. He treated his staff worse than any secular boss would have dared, waking us in the middle of the night or interrupting our family lives whenever the mood hit him. The offerings we took in went unaccounted for, and as Robert's lifestyle got more extravagant, his pleas for money during the church services grew shriller.

I knew he was wrong. I also knew there'd be the devil to pay if I said anything, as Robert would sooner behead you than tolerate criticism. So rather than confront, I appeased, refusing to speak up when I saw him lie, abuse, and manipulate the congregation. And the more of a prima donna he became, the less willing I was to even consider telling him the truth.

I finally slipped out and left, quietly and peacefully. But it was a false peace. I'd helped build the organization and then stood by passively while it crumpled into a tragedy.

Robert died twenty years ago, ravaged by AIDS contracted through the anonymous sexual encounters he began having while still in the pulpit.

None of his former staff members were surprised, but all of us, in my opinion, were guilty. We saw, and we did nothing.

WHY CONFRONT?

When you began The Game, God got your attention. Through repentance, confession, and discipline, you're hopefully not only maintaining your sobriety and developing a purer lifestyle, but you should also be developing a servant's heart. Two days ago, in fact, we discussed the need to rid yourself of the entitled mind-set—that old "Mine!" mentality—and strive for the greatness of servanthood.

That still holds true. But remember, at the beginning of this book we discussed the need to not only attain and maintain your purity, but also to attain, strengthen, and correct your relationships. And while correcting relationships usually means confessing *your* wrongdoing, at times it also means confronting someone else's wrongdoing. And that requires establishing, then protecting, personal boundaries.

In case you're wondering if this contradicts all we've said about service and humility, let me point out the Lord's teaching on boundaries and confrontation: "Moreover if your brother sins against you, go and tell him his fault between you and him alone. If he hears you, you have gained your brother. But if he will not hear, take with you one or two more, that 'by the mouth of two or three witnesses every word may be established.' And if he refuses to hear them, tell it to the church. But if he refuses even to hear the church, let him be to you like a heathen and a tax collector" (Matthew 18:15–17).

That's some confrontation! And notice, Jesus isn't just talking about someone who's sinned, but someone who's sinned *against you*. He's saying in clear terms that within the church, your close relations need to be guarded against unconfessed or unaddressed conflicts.

Here's where it gets tricky. A guy may be willing to confront someone who's in sin, remembering what Proverbs teaches about truth telling: "Open rebuke is better than love carefully concealed. Faithful are the wounds of a friend, but the kisses of an enemy are deceitful" (Proverbs 27:5–6). So if he knows a close friend or family member is doing something wrong, he'll confront the person.

But when that same friend or family member does something wrong to him *personally*, he freezes up, suddenly plagued with doubts: "Do I have the right to be angry about this? Who am I to say anything? Aren't I supposed to just shut up and take it?" Under the misguided notion that sins committed against him are sins he's supposed to ignore, he refuses to confront the wrongs.

That doesn't end the hurt he feels over them, though. It affects the way he sees the other person and the way he views the relationship itself. So with time it deteriorates as he becomes bitter, withdrawn, and weary of the person he's refusing to be honest with.

But if the average man feels self-conscious confronting, for the Player it may be downright unthinkable. He sees himself not just as a sinner, after all, but a *sexual* one, no less! His shame over being an adulterer or pornographer makes him feel he's in the "outcast" category, unqualified to say anything, even if he's being routinely stepped on.

I've seen this with husbands, for example, whose wives have caught them cheating or using porn. The wife is angry and hurt, as she should be. But she may also go overboard with her rage, humiliating him and throwing his sin in his face whenever the mood strikes her. When he offers a feeble protest, she jerks his chain with the old, "Hey, buddy, you're the sleazeball with the sexual problem, so don't even *think* of correcting me!"

If this goes on, he's setting himself up for resentment, and resentment is a setup for relapse.

All of this can be remedied with boundaries and, when need be, confrontation. So today, in the interest of correcting unhealthy patterns, we'll look at both.

BOUNDARIES ARE GOD-ORDAINED

Boundaries are terms that define what's allowable, and *not* allowable, in any relationship. And they are always established when God interacts with man.

In both Old and New Testaments, when God reveals Himself to a group or an individual, the rules are laid out. Read the Mosaic Law, for example, or the Sermon on the Mount or most of the New Testament. All of them include clear explanations of what God expects from man. Terms are also laid out for human relations: family roles, sexual limitations, business practices, social justice. Clearly, then, God places a high premium on boundaries and confronts His people when they cross them, either with Him or with each other.

That's because "God is not the author of confusion" (1 Corinthians 14:33), and confusion is guaranteed if boundaries are unclear or disrespected.

Compare this to driving, and you'll see my point. When we get on the road, we assume certain boundaries are understood and agreed on by all the other drivers. Stop signs, traffic signals, divider lines, and speed limits are all supposed to be respected; and if they're not, there'll be chaos, maybe even fatalities. It's impossible to drive safely and consistently without boundaries.

It's likewise impossible to sustain safe, healthy intimacy without boundaries. When we relate, whether to close friends, spouses, or family members, we assume certain rules will be understood and agreed on, like mutual respect, fairness, and consideration. If they're not, there'll be chaos and, in the worst cases, relational fatalities.

All of this makes establishing or renegotiating boundaries crucial to you. As you correct the way you're relating—that is, as you become more honest, patient, and consistent—you might also become aware of problems in your marriage, friendships, or business relations that also need correcting. And that may be the time to confront a long-term problem.

WHAT TO CONFRONT

When Jesus said, "If your brother sins against you, go and tell him" (Matthew 18:15), He allowed some leeway. In every relationship, after all, the person you're dealing with sins against you, and many of the sins we commit in marriage or friendship can (and should) be endured without comment. Our spouse may be late; our friend misses an appointment; someone we love might get irritable and a little abrupt. These are all sins, sure, but they hardly warrant an intervention. Remember, part of our responsibility in any relationship is to show patience and forgiveness, as Paul wrote: "Walk worthy of the calling with which you were called, with all lowliness and gentleness, with longsuffering, bearing with one another in love" (Ephesians 4:1–2).

Generally, then, we're called to a noncritical, gentle approach, especially toward our friends and family. But at times, someone's behavior may either be so *seriously* wrong or so *consistently* wrong that it needs pointing out. This is especially true if the behavior is seriously damaging the relationship—maybe even causing it to fall apart. In cases like that, you're not doing the other person any favors by allowing him or her to continue in that sin. In fact, you eventually become a partner in it, because while you are always responsible for what you do, you're also at times responsible for what you allow.

But since the Bible doesn't provide a list showing which sins to definitely confront and which ones to give a pass to, let me take a little liberty here. I've listed below twelve behaviors I've seen displayed by friends, wives, or family members of men I've worked with. When these behaviors have gone unchecked, the damage done has been immeasurable. So if any of the following are regularly coming up between you and someone you're close to, then I'd seriously suggest that a confrontation is called for:

1. Consistent and repeated name-calling or obscenities
2. Humiliation in front of others, during which you're yelled at or criticized, or in which personal information about you is discussed
3. Persistent dishonesty
4. Persistent rejections of your affection and interest
5. Teasing that demeans you, after you've asked the other person to stop it
6. Gossip or other behaviors that divide relationships
7. Repeating and rehashing your past sins, even after you've confessed and repented of them
8. Intrusion into parts of your life the other person hasn't been invited into
9. Refusal to honor terms that have already been agreed on
10. Financial defrauding
11. Sexually inappropriate behavior of any sort
12. Physical violence in any form

If these apply, the next step is to prayerfully and responsibly address them.

How to Confront

First, before confronting, *examine yourself.* Remember Jesus's warning: "And why do you look at the speck in your brother's eye, but do not consider the plank in your own eye? Or how can you say to your brother, 'Let me remove the speck from your eye'; and look, a plank is in your own eye? Hypocrite! First remove the plank from your own eye, and then you will see clearly to remove the speck from your brother's eye" (Matthew 7:3–5).

He didn't say you *shouldn't* address that plank in another's eye. He only directed you to start with yourself, since you can't see clearly to correct another person if your own vision is clouded.

So be sure you've looked at, confessed, and dealt with your shortcomings. In all fairness, the person you confront may know about your sexual struggles and may rightfully wonder why, at this time in your life, you're concentrating on his or her sins, rather than your own.

Second, before confronting, *get some additional wisdom.* Discuss this with your pastor or accountability partner or group. Tell them what the problem is in the relationship, how it's affecting you, and how you want to deal with it. Get some feedback from them before proceeding by asking some relevant questions:

1. I really feel I need to confront a problem with (person's name). This is what this person has been doing, and this is how it's been affecting me.

2. Does this person's behavior, in your opinion, warrant a confrontation? Or am I making too much of it?

3. Here are the points I want to make in this confrontation. Do they sound clear to you?

4. How does my attitude seem?

5. Are there any other points I should make or issues I should raise?

Third, when confronting someone, *be yourself.* You don't have to charge in like Rambo when you confront someone, so don't concern yourself with how aggressive you look or how strong you need to be. When confronting, the goal is clarity, not volume. Be sure you know what you're going to say, and don't concern yourself with how forcefully you say it.

Then, when it's time to have the "big conversation," let me suggest a simple five-point confrontation plan I've used over the years.

STATE YOUR INTENTION

"You matter so much—that's why we're talking."

Make sure the person knows you want your relationship to improve, and that she or he is so important to you that you hate for anything to come between the two of you.

Explain that you've been working on yourself and the sin in your own life and will continue to do so. But there's also an ongoing problem you've got to address.

STATE THE PROBLEM

"This is what you've been doing that I wish you wouldn't" or, "This is what you haven't been doing that I wish you would."

Be as precise as possible. Don't talk about generalities (as in, "You're rude to me" or, "You're demeaning me"), but stick to specifics. Try to give at least three examples of the behavior that's causing the problem, and make the examples as recent as possible.

STATE THE RESULT

"Our relationship is changing."

Let this person know the effect her or his behavior is having on you and what it's done to your relationship. Example: "I'm losing respect for you, and we're drifting apart" or, "My heart's hardening toward you even though I don't want it to."

STATE YOUR REQUEST

"This is what I need you to do in the future."

Again, be very specific. Tell the person you're not asking for him or her to feel bad. You're asking instead for changed behavior in the future.

This, by the way, is a good time to level the playing field a bit. When you're confronting someone, the other person almost always feels a bit defensive. No matter how polite you try to be, they'll usually feel as if you're calling them on the carpet, since you're the one with the complaint. Try to show good faith, by showing that you're not just trying to control the relationship, but that you're wanting it to improve.

A way to show goodwill, then, is to explain: "By the way, I know I'm far from being the perfect husband/friend/partner, so maybe there are some things I've been doing that have bothered you as well. Since we're being so horribly honest, why not tell me about them?"

This shows you're not interested in being morally superior and that the other person's feelings and needs really do matter to you.

STATE THE CONSEQUENCES OF IGNORING YOUR REQUEST

"This is where I think we're headed if things don't change."

This should never be presented as a threat but as an honest concern about the future of the relationship.

Hopefully, the person you're having this discussion with will be open to your ideas and will want to work with you toward better boundaries and policies. Often, though, that's not the case. A person may resist you either by denying what you're saying, minimizing its importance, or showing complete indifference to it.

In cases like that, you may need to point out the following:

1. I can't make you change your behavior, but I hope you at least understand the damage that's being caused if you don't.

2. Even though right now you can't seem to see how important this is, I hope you'll think it over, and maybe we can talk about this again.

3. I'd like us to see a pastor or counselor together, because we're not getting anywhere with this. It looks like we need some outside help.

4. If things don't improve, I don't know what steps I'll need to take. I'll have to get some counsel for myself, pray on it, and think it over. I promise to try to do what's right, but I will have to do something, because this isn't acceptable.

Then if the person you're dealing with is still unwilling to talk with a third party, get some wise counsel for yourself. Learn how to deal with or, if necessary, work around a difficult relationship. It's not ideal, but it can be done.

Confrontation is, I believe, one of the hardest aspects of the training phase. In fact, to be honest, I hope it's one you'll be able to skip altogether. I hope you can skip it because the people in your life—your wife, family members, close friends, and fellow believers—are supportive and fair, so there's no one you need to go through all these steps with.

That's what I hope. But it's been my experience, unfortunately, that many Players are in some unhappy situations indeed.

Some have been emotionally passive and broken from early in life. They've spent years letting themselves be abused and taken for granted, so they've attracted and joined themselves with people who have very little respect for healthy boundaries.

Others are in marriages that were troubled long before their sexual sin came to light. Their home lives are volatile, and their marital life is a series of power struggles and endless debates over who's right.

Still others have so damaged and betrayed the people in their lives that they're now reaping an awful harvest of bitterness and hostility, which, sadly, they themselves have sown.

All these cases cry out for boundaries, although establishing them won't be easy. It'll be uphill, no doubt, as you continue to confront, negotiate, and pray for the person you're having difficulties with.

So as a Player in training, you'll need to keep up your flake resistance, because with confrontation, there often comes tension.

You'll be tempted to drop The Game entirely: too much hassle, too many problems, not enough energy. You'll want to flake by going back to the status quo, which is unhealthy but, at least, familiar.

Resist that urge, because you've come too far. By now you've corrected so many problems and adopted important lifestyle changes. This is no time to flake out just because you've hit a difficult emotional wall. Sowing in righteousness, while difficult, is never in vain: "Therefore do not cast away your confidence, which has great reward. For you have need of endurance, so that after you have done the will of God, you may receive the promise" (Hebrews 10:35–36).

I hope you'll always have the courage to confront your own wrongdoing. And, when necessary, I hope you'll draw on the additional courage to confront another's as well.

DAY 24

ACTION PLAN FOR DEVELOPING BOUNDARIES

KEY VERSE

Open rebuke is better than love carefully concealed. Faithful are the wounds of a friend, but the kisses of an enemy are deceitful.

—PROVERBS 27:5–6

PRINCIPLE

If you've been allowing your boundaries to be crossed by the people closest to you, you've been participating with them in their sin by enabling and encouraging it. Further, you've been blocking the intimacy that should be flowing between you and the people with whom you are in primary relationships. To correct this, you'll need to address your own passivity and confront someone else's behavior.

ACTION

Write or type into your own computer the answers to the following questions.

1. Who comes to mind when you think of someone routinely crossing your boundaries?
2. What is the nature of your relationship with this person (spouse, family member, friend)?
3. In general terms, what has this person's attitude toward you been?

4. In specific terms, what is this person repeatedly doing (or not doing) that's disrupting your relationship? Write down three recent examples.

5. At your next meeting with your accountability partner or group (or both) review questions one through four, and ask for their feedback. Do they feel your concerns are justified? Do they think you may be misreading the situation? Do they feel a loving confrontation is in order?

6. If they do not feel a confrontation is in order, ask them to clarify their reasons, so you can better understand how you may be misreading the situation.

7. If they do feel a confrontation is in order, set a date with this person within the next five days to discuss the situation with him or her, using the five-point confrontation plan outlined in Day 23.

RATIONALE

If there's an ongoing problem between you and someone you're close to, it will disrupt your ability to be intimate, harden your heart toward that person, discourage honest communication, and encourage personal passivity. As a Player, you're required to not only be a man of sexual integrity but of relational integrity as well. For this reason, unhealthy relational patterns in your life must be addressed.

PRAYER

Father, I've spent most of this process so far examining the log in my own eye, and that's as it should be. After all, there's been such an abundance of sin in my life that I'd be a fool to spend my energy focusing on someone else's.

But I also want to show integrity by having the courage to confront, when confrontation is Your will. So give me the wisdom to know what to say, the boldness to say it clearly, and the humility to say it as a servant and a friend. I ask this in Jesus's name. Amen.

GAME STATUS UPON COMPLETION OF
SECTION FOUR

By the end of Section Four (Training), you should have done the following: (Check off each item you've completed.)

_____ Learned and practiced the distraction technique for resisting visual temptations and discussed your progress in using this technique with your accountability group and partner.

_____ Learned and practiced the reality check technique for resisting long-term temptations and discussed your progress in using this technique with your accountability group and partner.

_____ Written out your recollections of at least five specific mercies God has shown you and how you think He's felt when you've forgotten or ignored those mercies.

_____ Written out your description of a man whose life is yielded as a living sacrifice to God.

_____ Determined if there is someone in your life whose behavior is consistently crossing your boundaries, and discussed this relationship with your accountability group and partner.

_____ If appropriate, set a date with this person to confront their behavior and work toward a healthier relationship.

If you've left any of these action items undone, go back and complete them before continuing to Section Five.

R Day 25   In Case of Relapse
           We develop a plan to follow in the event
           of relapse—a plan we hope we'll
           never use.

O Day 26   Action Plan for
           Relapse Contingency

   Day 27   Your Broader Purpose
           We examine the need for developing a
           sense of calling and purpose beyond
U   *sexual purity.*

   Day 28   Action Plan for
           Your Broader Purpose

T Day 29   Conversion and Epiphany
           We examine Peter's great failure and the
           converting effect it had on his service, his
           self-awareness, and his relationship
           with Christ.

ENDURANCE

   Day 30   Action Plan for Epiphany

DAY 25

IN CASE OF RELAPSE

*It is not the critic who counts . . . the credit belongs to the
man who is actually in the arena; who strives valiantly;
who errs and comes short again and again; and who, if he
fails, at least fails while daring greatly.*

—THEODORE ROOSEVELT

Sometimes my accountability partner, Trent, and I picture the
doomsday scenario of a relapse. It's morbid, imagining the ways
we'd handle it if we broke our sobriety, and we shudder when we
picture the outcome. Relapse is one of our worst nightmares, so at
times we ward it off by joking about it, the way people sometimes
joke about the Big One dropping—it *could* happen, but we're not
counting on it.

We consider the numbness we'd probably feel. It's been twenty
years since I used porn or committed fornication; just slightly less
than that for him. So after such a long sobriety stretch, we'd go
into shock.

Then there'd be our wives—what about coming clean to them?
We've both promised each other that we would tell our wives if we
ever slipped, but it would be a death sentence to so many things—
Renee's confidence in me, the exclusive bond we've shared, my
credibility as a father and husband. Thinking about it puts knots
in my stomach.

Who else would we tell? We're both in leadership, so there'd be
repercussions if we admitted having a sexual fall. I get extreme at
that point, telling Trent I'd just drop everything and go manage a

doughnut shop, hoping no one who'd known me as a pastoral counselor would drop by for a cinnamon roll.

Then we get more realistic and ask the tough questions. Is sobriety all that defines us? Does one transgression undo years of learning and growing? Or do we make too much of our goal of "staying sober for life"?

And inevitably, we decide that no, our sobriety's *not* all that defines us. We're Christians, husbands, fathers, and Americans— a relapse wouldn't undo these things.

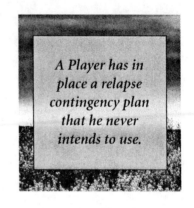

A Player has in place a relapse contingency plan that he never intends to use.

But it would mar them, and that's when sobriety takes on the right perspective. It isn't everything, but it *affects* everything. Nor does it define our life, but it enhances it. It's like my country—not everything, but much, and certainly worth fighting for.

Then we smile, shrug, take out our lists, and Trent says, "So this week, Joe, did you at any time . . ."

RELAPSE IS ALWAYS POSSIBLE, NEVER INEVITABLE

By today, if you've been following The Game Plan, you should have pursued an *ideal* and required a *standard* of yourself for at least twenty days.

You should be pursuing the ideal of sexual *purity*, which is a complete absence of any sexually sinful thought, word, or deed. Have you fallen short? Sure, I'll bet you've had a dirty thought here and there. But you're pursuing the ideal nonetheless, always striving for and achieving a higher level of inward and outward purity.

Sexual *sobriety* is no ideal, though. It's a standard you've been requiring of yourself, because you know you can meet it. It's reasonable to expect you won't use pornography or commit fornication or adultery; as a Christian, demanding anything less of yourself is ludicrous. And the number of days you've abstained make up that investment we call your sobriety. It's an investment that, I hope, you're committed to protecting.

Today, then, we'll discuss how to protect it and what to do if (God forbid) you should relapse. Relapse prevention and a contingency (what to do in case of relapse) are standard equipment for any Player.

GET CONFIDENT, NOT COCKY!

Relapse is always possible, but it's never inevitable. So learn to live with these two axioms, and give each of them the attention they're due.

You could always relapse, you know. As long as you have free will and opportunity—and you'll have both for as long as you're breathing—then a relapse is possible. Just because you rejected a sin doesn't mean you destroyed it. It still exists, and when you left it, it graciously said, "I'm here if you ever change your mind."

So if you do change your mind, you'll find backsliding to be a simple activity: just turn toward what you once turned from, then walk.

I hope you won't underestimate your ability to do so. The same apostle who wrote glowingly of victory and described us as "more than conquerors" was just as emphatic about proper caution: "Therefore let him who thinks he stands take heed lest he fall" (Romans 8:37; 1 Corinthians 10:12).

I'm a sucker for Sylvester Stallone's *Rocky* series, which chronicles the ups and downs of champion boxer Rocky Balboa. And I know of no better cinematic example of 1 Corinthians 10:12 than one that appears early in *Rocky III*.

By this point in the story, Balboa's an undisputed champ, wealthy and famous, and he has accepted a challenge to fight a hungry underdog named Clubber Lang. Certain he'll wipe the floor with Lang, Rocky gets, well, *cocky*. He's in dynamite shape, but he trains more like a pretty boy than a fighter. The camera zooms in on Clubber training like an animal, then shows Balboa halfheartedly skipping rope in his gym, accompanied by a live band, pausing to kiss a fan or sign an autograph in the middle of his workout.

He's come so far he thinks he can't lose, so he's casual about his training. Shortly, he learns a terrible lesson.

But you don't need to. Even when you're undefeated—that is, sober and pressing on in purity and strength—there's still opportunity to sin, you'll still at times be susceptible to compromise, and you've still got an opponent itching to take you down. So take heed and train seriously even when you're on a winning streak. (Did I say *even* when you're on a winning streak? Scratch that—I meant *especially* when you're on a winning streak!)

But train with confidence. Just because you *could* relapse doesn't mean you *have* to. Especially now, because if you're following this program, you've got tools, allies, insight, and support. So there's no reason for you to relapse. You're susceptible to temptations, yes. But susceptible and helpless are two very different things.

So don't relapse. You don't have to; you don't want to. And hasn't enough happened already? You've been through the wringer over your sexual sin one too many times, so give yourself and the people who love you a break. Don't relapse.

Relapse Setups

To avoid relapse, you should be aware of the situations, states of mind, or wrong decisions that could make you more susceptible to a relapse. I call these relapse setups, because they can set you up to fall.

Let's look at a few of these today, in hopes you'll remember them and stay beyond their reach.

PROGRAM NEGLECT

I think this is the most common setup. Most relapses I've seen haven't occurred for complicated, obscure reasons. They've happened because someone neglected his program. He simply got lazy and stopped praying, studying Scripture, attending meetings, and working on his maintenance routine.

By nature, we're not prone to stick to anything. Jesus pointed this out in the parable of the sower, where He showed that most people who received the Word had a brief, temporary response to it without long-term follow-through (Matthew 13:3–8). Likewise, most of the churches He addressed in the Revelation started well but had degenerated (Revelation 2–3), and most of Paul's friends and co-workers let him down toward the end of his life (2 Timothy 4:9–16). Inconsistency is a common downfall.

But it needn't be. If you'll be reconciled to two unchanging facts about yourself, you can avoid this setup.

First, you will relapse if you don't stick to your daily and weekly structure. Period. No exceptions. Your heart and mind need the influences the structure provides, and nothing can replace that.

Second, it takes only a moderate amount of effort to stick with this program. Fifteen minutes a day for disciplines, a couple of hours a week for accountability. That's moderate, and you can handle it. So give yourself no excuses for program neglect.

TRIUMPHALISM:
MISTAKING ABSENCE OF SYMPTOMS FOR CURE

Theologically, "triumphalism" is a teaching that overemphasizes the triumphant aspects of faith without recognizing the reality of human struggle. So triumphalist teaching would have you believe that God wants you rich, healthy, and problem free and that anything short of that is second-rate Christianity. It's a cruel doctrine because, when presented to a woman with cancer or a child who's born into terrible poverty, it suggests that if only they had more faith, their problems would disappear.

In recovery, triumphalism takes on a different, though similar, form. It suggests that if you've gotten better, you must be cured and no longer in need of disciplines or accountability. And whereas many people neglect their programs through sheer laziness or inconsistency, the triumphalist rejects it entirely because he thinks he's arrived.

I saw this repeatedly when I was a case manager in an inpatient psychiatric hospital. A patient would be admitted during a psychotic episode and need immediate medication and stabilizing. So he'd be put on the proper drugs, get individual and group counseling, and develop some better coping skills. Within days, his symptoms would diminish, and he would say, "I'm cured! Thanks much, I don't need this anymore."

And with that, he'd discharge himself, against his doctor's advice, and take himself off his medications. Within days, he'd be back, starting the cycle again.

And all because he thought improvement meant cure. He thought he didn't need his meds because he was getting better. Yet the fact that he was getting better was proof that the meds *were* working and that he *did* need them!

No doubt you'll improve if you stick to your meds. Stay in the Word, develop your bonds with God in prayer, stay accountable, and exercise more impulse control, and you'll see genuine, lasting change. But when the change comes, recognize why it came. It came because the program you're following is working, and if it's working, why abandon it?

The apostle Paul himself said he hadn't arrived: "Not that I have already attained, or am already perfected; but I press on, that I may lay hold of that for which Christ Jesus has also laid hold of me" (Philippians 3:12). I guess we'd be wise to say the same. Improving but imperfect; growing though not fully grown; pressing on yet not arrived—that's us.

UNWILLINGNESS TO CONFESS STRUGGLES

I hope we're clear on the difference between a struggle and a transgression. A transgression is a willful act of disobedience; a struggle is a temptation to commit that act. When I struggle, I'm tempted. When I transgress, I act.

I'm expected not to transgress, and that's fair. I can choose not to relapse; I can choose to avoid relapse setups. But I can't choose not to struggle. I'll be tempted, sometimes ferociously, sometimes mildly. And that puts me in the company of every saint who walks on this fallen ground.

But sometimes we forget that, especially when we know people are watching us and rooting for us. When the people you love see you reclaiming created intent, they often want the best for you. They want your story to be victorious and glowing; and let's face it—we all love seeing a sinner find redemption. So nobody can blame your family and friends for wanting you to do well.

Yet the desire to please others can override the need for honesty. This leads many a married man, for example, to present himself to his wife in a somewhat idealized light.

"How are you doin', honey?" she'll ask. She knows he goes to support group once a week and meets with his accountability partner, and she's dying to know what they discuss. But she respects his privacy and leaves it to him to volunteer any important details. Still, she's anxious. He's slipped in the past, and she wants, occasionally, some reassurance. "Any problems?" she asks. "Any temptations?"

He knows the answer she's hoping to hear. He's disappointed her in the past, and he'd love nothing more than to make her feel secure and safe. The truth is, he's sober, better, and occasionally tempted. That's not so bad; it's just not ideal. And oh, how he wants to give her ideal! So he hedges, just a bit: "Great, babe. No temptations, not a one. No problems."

It seems a small compromise; and in the scheme of things, I suppose it is. It avoids needless worries on her part and conveniently lets him off the hook. But here's the problem: if you start lying in one area, you'll redevelop the habit of lying in all areas. Remember Paul's take on leaven: "Do you not know that a little leaven leavens the whole lump?" (1 Corinthians 5:6).

A little lying expands quickly into full-scale cover-ups and deceptions, because lying gives you the luxury of avoiding the uncomfortable truth. And lying is one sin you cannot avoid to flirt with, because it's a sin that protects, strengthens, and enhances sexual acting out.

If and when you struggle, admit it. If and when you improve, celebrate it. Above all, keep it real. "Real" isn't always pretty, but ultimately it's safer than "ideal" can ever be.

UNWILLINGNESS TO ADDRESS DEEPER ISSUES

Years ago, I leased office space in a charming, old historical building in our city. It was a three-story affair with nooks and crannies
everywhere, including a basement and, beneath the basement, a
crawlspace for storage. Several different counselors and attorneys
practiced there, and all of us were proud of the building's rustic
charm.

Until the day we walked in and got a whiff of something indescribably nauseating. We couldn't tell where it was coming from,
but it permeated the place. We opened all the windows to air the
rooms out, then searched every bathroom and trash can in the
building to find whatever it was that was causing such a stink.

No luck. We sprinkled scented dust on the carpet to mask the
odors, which got stronger as the day progressed, and by the next
morning, we seriously feared our clients would refuse to come in
until we got rid of that smell.

By then, it was obvious to us it came from the basement. Worse
yet, it came from the crawlspace under the basement, a tiny area
that was dark and mysterious. None of us wanted to crawl under
there and see what the problem was, so we endured another two
days of the smell until there was no choice but to pay someone to
dive into that dark place and locate the problem.

We hired a handyman, who solved the mystery. A stray cat had
found its way under the house and, for whatever reason, had died
there. The carcass was the problem which, when removed, solved
the problem of the odor.

A man's heart can also be a dark, scary place. Jeremiah described
it this way: "The heart is deceitful above all things, and desperately
wicked. Who can know it?" (Jeremiah 17:9) Deep resentment, old
wounds, and unspoken fears can lodge deep in the heart, hiding
and festering. They, too, can give off an odor through a man's
behavior and attitude.

The behavior may really stink, causing people to notice and
demand he do something about it. And he may, by stopping the
behavior without addressing the problem of the heart that led to

it. But that's what we did when we sprinkled the scented powder on the carpet, only to find it could mask the odor, but not eliminate it.

By all means stop the acting out. It's unacceptable and is, in and of itself, a huge problem. But it may also be the symptom of a larger, more deeply hidden problem as well. If so, you'll never solve it without taking some time to dive into that uninviting crawlspace and deal with the carcass that's stuck inside.

Relapse Contingency

I hesitate whenever I speak on relapse contingency, because invariably someone will ask, "Does this mean a relapse has to happen? If you're telling me what to do in case of a relapse, aren't you telling me I *will* relapse?"

No, not at all. A contingency is something you put in place *in case* something happens, not because it *will* happen.

You see contingencies all around you. In most public buildings, you'll find glass cases marked "In Case of Fire, Break Glass." No one is saying a fire *will* happen—they're only saying that if it does, certain equipment is available. When you ride the elevator, there's a number posted by the floor buttons, indicating who to call in case you get stuck. No one's saying you *will* get stuck, but if you do, they want you to be prepared.

And, no, I don't think you'll relapse. In fact, I'm confident I'm about to give you some suggestions you'll never have to use. But I'd be remiss not to suggest them anyway. Since relapse is a sad but real possibility, I would rather you have a plan in place if it does happen, rather than flounder around wondering what to do (or what not to do) after it happens.

John seems to have been writing something along these lines when he said, "My little children, these things I write to you, so that you may not sin. And if anyone sins, we have an Advocate with the Father; Jesus Christ the righteous" (1 John 2:1).

Notice the wording: "I write to you, so that you may not sin."

He's saying, "Don't sin—you don't have to. I'm writing to help you avoid it." But, he adds, if you do sin, there's still hope. We have an Advocate, even when we sin.

So it is with a relapse contingency plan. Don't relapse. But if you do, take these steps immediately:

NOTIFY

Decide now who you'd call if you relapsed. In most cases your accountability partner is your best bet, since he works with you weekly and you're probably in regular contact with him. But a member of your group will also be a good choice, or perhaps a pastor or counselor. What matters is that you know who to call and what number to use, and that you call him immediately. Tell him that you relapsed and that you'll need his prayers and support. If you have a severe crisis situation, meet with him ASAP. Otherwise, you can discuss this more at your next group or individual meeting.

The longer you wait to call him, the more tempted you'll be to cover up the relapse and never deal with it. And that, as you know, will lead you right back to the lying and covering up that helped create the problem in the first place.

IDENTIFY

With the help of whomever you notify, figure out what went wrong. Usually, as I said before, people relapse because they slacked off on their program. But there may be other reasons, so spend time exploring what you were doing before the relapse, what you could have done differently, and what you'll do differently in the future to prevent this from happening again. Human error is a terrific textbook, so you may as well use it.

MOVE IT!

Get back into your program immediately, and start recounting your sobriety days. You'll accomplish nothing by wallowing in grief over your relapse, and there's no reason to delay beginning again. If you refuse to start over, you're yielding to a more severe, deadlier sin than relapse: despair. Sexual sin you can repent of, but despair? Yield to that, and you're really finished.

Don't be. Relapse is a temporary setback; despair is the end.

You're protecting a treasure when you guard your sobriety, so apply yourself to its longevity the way you'd protect a valuable antique or piece of jewelry. Recognizing its worth, you work both to keep it and to keep it in its best possible shape.

Playing The Game, likewise, is a purposeful, challenging, exciting way to live; and keeping the ball (your sobriety) is worth all the blood, sweat, and tears a committed athlete has to shed.

Yet, as I hope to show in our last few days together, there are even more important things in life than your sobriety. Guard it, treasure it, and then keep pressing on. Because as fine an achievement as it is, there's certainly life beyond sobriety.

DAY 26

ACTION PLAN FOR RELAPSE CONTINGENCY

KEY VERSE

My little children, these things I write to you, so that you may not sin. And if anyone sins, we have an Advocate with the Father, Jesus Christ the righteous.

—1 JOHN 2:1

PRINCIPLE

To relapse is to break sobriety—a very serious event, and one you want to avoid. So first and foremost, you want to prevent relapse. Still, you should be prepared for (without giving yourself permission for) a relapse contingency. A relapse contingency is the plan of action you've put in place in case of relapse.

ACTION

1. Write or type into your computer the name and number of the person you'd call in the event of a relapse. This should be your accountability partner, although you may choose someone else if you prefer, provided that person knows he's your "emergency call."

2. If you're married, discuss with your accountability partner what your disclosure policy with your wife will be if you relapse.

3. Of the four relapse setups mentioned in Day 26—program neglect, triumphalism, unwillingness to disclose struggles, or unwillingness to address deeper issues—which do you think you'd be most prone to? Why do you feel you'd be prone to it?

RATIONALE

Good relapse prevention includes both a prevention plan and a contingency to follow in the event of a relapse. For that reason, you need to have both your structures and policies in place in advance, so in the event of a crisis, there'll be little or no guesswork as to what you should do.

PRAYER

Father, in taking this action plan, I'm putting together a structure I fervently pray I will never have to use. But as a steward who's failed in the past, I know that failure is possible, though not inevitable. Help me guard the sobriety You've enabled me to build up so far, and remind me, when I'm tempted to make compromises that might lead to a relapse, just how much I have to lose and how little benefit I'd gain in return. I ask this in Jesus's name. Amen.

DAY 27

YOUR BROADER PURPOSE

*Until you give yourself permission to be the unique person
God made you to be . . . and to do the unpredictable
things grace allows you to do—you will march around in
vicious circles of fear, timidity, and boredom. It's time to
stop marching and start flying.*

—CHUCK SWINDOLL, THE FINISHING TOUCH

I needed an internship. I'd made an appointment with my school's administrator, who was checking her files for any recent openings. She found one and pulled it out. "Here's a small Christian counseling center taking trainees."

"What kind of counseling do they do?" I asked, not really caring. Students have to take what's available.

She glanced at the file, raising her eyebrows. "Well, it's not mainstream. They deal with sexual addiction, marital problems, homosexuality, and sexual dysfunction."

"I'd rather flip burgers!" I snapped. She looked up at me, startled and taken aback. She knew about my history, as we'd had several long talks during the year. She said, "I'd really like you to take this one, Joe. You could bring a lot of your own experience into it, and the best counselors are the ones who speak from experience."

"How long would they need me?"

"Six months, then you can sign on again if you'd like."

"OK," I sighed. "I'll try it for six months. Six months of counseling people who are—what? What do I call these clients?"

"People like you."

"Fine, people like me. Six months, that's it. Then I look into something else, anything else."

That was March 1987. I never did find anything else.

A Player pursues his passion and calling beyond sexual purity.

PLAYING WITH A PURPOSE

In this book's introduction, I said that when playing The Game, you have five primary goals. Since we're just four days away from finishing our thirty days together, let's review these goals and see if they've been reached.

TO ABSTAIN FROM THE SEXUAL SIN THAT HAS DOMINATED YOU

On Day 6 you should have made the final cut with the behavior that has dominated you and disrupted your life. You should have separated yourself from it as much as possible and informed (within the same week) at least one person about the action you'd just taken.

Following that, you should have developed daily structure (Day 8), weekly accountability (Day 10), and a better understanding of temptation and response (Day 18).

With that structure and accountability, you should be able to abstain even when the pull toward the behavior is strong.

Ask yourself three questions:

1. Have I taken these steps?

2. Have I abstained?

3. If not, why not?

TO REPAIR DAMAGED RELATIONSHIPS AND MAKE RESTITUTION

You should also have, if necessary, made restitution to anyone injured by your behavior by acknowledging what you'd done and the impact your behavior has had on that person (Day 12).

Ask yourself three questions:

1. Have I taken these steps?

2. Has this relationship improved?

3. If not, why not?

TO MAINTAIN A PERMANENT STRUCTURE OF DISCIPLINE AND ACCOUNTABILITY

On Days 8 and 10, you should have established both. Day 10's action plan may have taken a week to accomplish, since you had to research available groups, but by now your accountability should be in place.

Ask yourself three questions:

1. Are my disciplines in place?

2. Is my accountability in place?

3. If not, why not?

TO SUCCESSFULLY MANAGE SEXUAL TEMPTATIONS WHEN THEY ARISE

On Days 17 through 20, you studied and began practicing resistance techniques. You should have practiced them privately on Days 19 and 20, and by now you should have had some chances to use them in your daily routine. They're still new to you, but you should be practicing them regularly by now.

Ask yourself three questions:

1. Have I learned the resistance techniques?

2. Have I incorporated them into my routine?

3. If not, why not?

TO CORRECT UNHEALTHY WAYS OF RELATING

On Days 15 and 16, you studied and took action, as necessary, on personal wounds. Then, on Days 21 through 24, you studied and, as needed, took action on the problem of entitlement and the need to confront if someone is routinely and seriously crossing your boundaries.

If you've needed to contact someone to discuss unresolved problems (see Day 16) or to confront current relational problems (see Day 24), you may not, at this point, have been able to have the necessary conversation with this person. But by now you should have determined *if* there's someone you need to contact; where and how you're going to discuss the problem; and whom you're going to get some advice and insight from before having this conversation.

Ask yourself three questions:

1. Have I learned these steps?

2. Have I taken them?

3. If not, why not?

If there are any of these five primary goals you still haven't reached, go back to the day (or days) connected with the goal. Read the lesson for that day again, then do the action plan. Do that now, before finishing the rest of this book.

But if by now you *have* taken all of these steps, then congratulations! I knew you could. You've probably found, as I have, that none of these steps are huge. But when taken together, they have a huge effect, don't they? Keep it up, and keep moving ahead, because if you've gotten this far, you've played well.

Now let's talk about life beyond these steps.

MAN'S SEARCH FOR MEANING

Israel's release from Egypt is often called their deliverance. God saw their misery and was moved to action. But remember, it was not just a deliverance *from* but a deliverance *to*. God freed them from hard servitude, and that alone was deliverance. But it was also a means to an end, the end being the Promised Land. There, they'd make new conquests, establish their homes, develop their community, and enjoy a better life.

God looked on you, too, hating not just the sexual sin in your life but its enslaving quality. It limited you, whether you realized it or not, and you, too, were in servitude: "His own iniquities entrap the wicked man, and he is caught in the cords of his sin" (Proverbs 5:22).

So He interrupted your life to provoke a release, and it worked. But leaving your personal Egypt isn't enough for Him, nor should it be for you. Having turned from it, you turn toward new conquests, community, and meaning.

Meaning—there's a packed word! Rick Warren's excellent *The Purpose Driven Life* has sold twenty million copies (as of this writing) largely because it speaks plainly to our need for purpose, and the emptiness of life without one.[15]

Nearly fifty years ago, psychiatrist Viktor Frankl, a Holocaust survivor who endured Auschwitz, wrote on the same theme in his book *Man's Search for Meaning*.[16] Dr. Frankl observed during his imprisonment that the inmates most likely to survive the horrors of the camps were the ones with a clear and deeply held sense of meaning—a goal, vision, or cause that was worth fighting and surviving for. And while many of Frankl's views are by no means biblical, his observations on meaning were keen. Without purpose, an affluent executive despairs; with purpose, a starved and beaten soul in a concentration camp holds on.

Then there's you, a man who's established lifestyle changes and is building deeper intimacy with God and others. Good start, but there's still the question of a broader purpose, because there's more to your life than sexual purity. In fact, I'll bet by now you're sick of hearing yourself referred to as a "sinner," "a man in recovery," or even "a Player." And you might, as I did, simply want to put this behind you and (besides discussing it with your accountability partner and group) never mention it again.

I don't blame you. But first, at least think through what you're learning about God, life, yourself, and others through all of this, and see what might be worth passing on. You may have picked up information that's relevant and very useful to others.

Something out of the book of Exodus hit me a few months back. When God was laying down laws about civil and religious life (lots of boundaries, remember?), He mentioned strangers—foreigners who interacted with the Israelites. And this commandment stood out to me: "You shall neither mistreat a stranger nor oppress him, for you were strangers in the land of Egypt" (Exodus 22:21). "Remember what it was like," God was saying, "and let that memory influence the way you treat a stranger."

I'm glad you've left Egypt; but for better or worse, you'll always remember it. It taught you what it's like to be bound by something that corrupts the most valuable parts of your life. It taught you about shame, deceit, compromise, fear, and secrecy; it was a lesson in grace, reconciliation, new beginnings, and humility as well. Isn't there something in all of that worth passing on? And isn't there a stranger somewhere who could use it?

Rick Warren makes this point in *The Purpose Driven Life*: "The second part of your life message is the truths that God has taught you from experiences with him. These are lessons and insights you have learned about God, relationships, problems, temptations, and other aspects of life." (Didn't know he wrote a bestseller about you, did you?) "Of course, you have many other testimonies," he continues. "You have a story for *every* experience in which God has helped you . . . Be sensitive and use the story."[17]

I learned, back when I reluctantly accepted that internship, that the part of my life I was the most ashamed of was the very thing equipping me to be of some real use to others. And while I don't think every Christian who has overcome sexual sin needs to go out and start a ministry, I'm convinced you'll find opportunities, if you prayerfully watch for them, to take this struggle and convert it into something that equips and encourages others.

That's what I call a redemptive response to tragedy, and it's not uncommon.

Chuck Colson did it with his own disgrace in the wake of Watergate. After falling from a key post with the Nixon administration to a federal prison, Colson converted the darkest time of his life into the effective, thriving ministry known as Prison Fellowship.

Jim Bakker, former president of PTL Ministries, did the same after his own public humiliation. When his prior adultery came to light and his ministry collapsed amid financial scandal, Bakker endured divorce, then prison time. Released years later, he wrote his memoirs *I Was Wrong*, gleaning wisdom from his failure and passing it on.[18]

My favorite example, though, is the late Corrie ten Boom. You may have read her book *The Hiding Place* or seen the movie of the same name. During World War II, the Ten Booms sheltered Jews in Holland and were eventually turned over to the Gestapo to pay the ultimate price. Many in her family soon died, and Corrie and her sister were sent to jail, then on to Germany to the notorious Ravensbrück concentration camp.

More than once I heard her speak about it, noting that as awful as it was, she'd never felt God's presence and guidance as she did during that time. She smuggled a Bible into the camp, where she and her sister ministered evangelism and comfort in the middle of hell. Her sister eventually took ill and, while dying, told Corrie they must tell people what they'd learned in the camp. "They'll believe us," she said, "because we've been there." Corrie ten Boom went on to become one of the most beloved of modern saints, with a staggering message and ministry born of her worst experiences.

Now fast-forward to the church in the twenty-first century. Are we not, among other things, a church in moral crisis? If we look not only at the discouraging statistics I cited early in this book on moral failure among Christians, but also at recent well-known scandals among Christian leadership, what do we see if not a church that is seriously compromised?

In response, God is intervening, as more and more of His men experience His wake-up call, just as you did. And that makes you part of a moral reformation He's doing in the church today.

As members of the body of Christ reclaim created intent, the church is strengthened and better able to respond to the women and men who come from the sexually idolatrous culture—the strangers, you could say—looking for answers. On this point, Episcopal bishop William Fry noted: "One of the most attractive features of the early Christian communities was their radical sexual ethic and their deep commitment to family values. These things drew many people to them who were disillusioned by the promiscuity of what proved to be a declining culture."[19]

If the early church's commitment to family values attracted those burnt out on the excesses of their time, imagine the potential of today's church! How much further can the sexual revolution go before its members—the promiscuous, the pornographers, the homosexuals—burn out and start looking for another alternative? Will they not be the new "strangers" seeking answers and understanding?

More to the point: who will be better equipped to *provide* answers and understanding than those of us who've struggled with our own sexual excesses?

Let's think over what we've learned from playing The Game. It may become the textbook we draw on when broken men come to us, wounded and disillusioned by their own Egypt.

There's meaning in that. We'll have something to say to them.

And they'll believe us, because we've been there.

DAY 28

ACTION PLAN FOR YOUR BROADER PURPOSE

KEY VERSE

Therefore, brethren, be even more diligent to make your call and election sure, for if you do these things you will never stumble; for so an entrance will be supplied to you abundantly into the everlasting kingdom of our Lord and Savior Jesus Christ.

—2 PETER 1:10–11

PRINCIPLE

Your repentance was a means to an end. It was first necessary that you "leave Egypt" by abandoning the behavior that had you in bondage. But now you've got to give serious consideration to Canaan—the Promised Land—where your long-term future lies.

ACTION

1. Read Galatians 1:11–24. Notice Paul's life as an apostle began when he was interrupted by God; then with time his calling became clearer to him, being confirmed by experience, passion, and others.

2. What are the current responsibilities you have that you're certain God has given you and commissioned you to oversee (such as family, business, other responsibilities)? If they're God-given, you need to *keep* and *protect* them.

3. What are you currently doing—in your work, church life, volunteer life, or hobby—that you feel *passionate* about?

4. Is there anything you feel a passion to do that you're not doing? Why? What are your specific reasons for not pursuing it?

5. What gifts do you feel you have to offer the body of Christ?

6. What opportunities are there for you to use these gifts?

RATIONALE

Determining your broader purpose requires introspection, insight, and feedback from others. By answering the questions above, you should get an idea of what specific gifts you have to offer, where your heart and passions lie, and what opportunities you may or may not be using to bring a greater sense of meaning into your life.

PRAYER

Father, as I look around I see more opportunities than I could possibly respond to, more needs than I can meet, more worthy causes than I could ever support. I'm willing, Lord, to put my efforts into any of them, but the question remains: what would You have me to do?

I need wisdom. Help me discern the passions of my heart that may have been dormant for years. Help me identify the gifts You've given me, that I might be a good and faithful steward of them. Help me see the opportunities You would have me pursue, and make it clear to me where I fit into Your plans and purposes for the times You've placed me in. I ask this in Jesus's name. Amen.

DAY 29

CONVERSION AND EPIPHANY

At the moment when he exclaimed "I am a scoundrel!" he
had seen himself as he really was . . . his past life, his first
fault, his liberation . . . all this recurred to him, but in a
light which he had never before seen.
He looked at his life, and it appeared to him horrible; at
his soul, and it appeared to him frightful.
Still, a soft light was shed over both . . .

—VICTOR HUGO, LES MISÉRABLES

History is, among other things, a series of interventions—man errs;
God interrupts him. Interruption then leads to correction, correction leads to redemption, man compromises again, and the cycle
renews itself. Life is hopeless without the divine interruption.

That's what got you into The Game. Whatever your sexual compromise was, it was no match for God's plans. He'd already named
and chosen you, and He was determined to accomplish a purpose in
you. That purpose was established before the foundations of the
world were laid, and He wasn't about to let it be thwarted. So
through a crisis of truth, He got your attention, and you got pulled
over (a pit stop, remember, not the junkyard) for a five-part process:
repentance, order, understanding, training, and endurance.

The crisis generated either the fear or anger needed to motivate
you to action, so you turned away from something or someone.
You separated yourself from what had become unacceptable and
removed, as much as possible, the opportunity to return to it. You
repented—praise God!—and got into The Game.

Then you turned toward Him. You developed or redeveloped intimacy with God, hearing from Him daily through His Word, and speaking to Him daily in prayer. You knew love for Him would translate into obedience and that to know Him is to love Him. So you began devoting yourself to knowing and loving God.

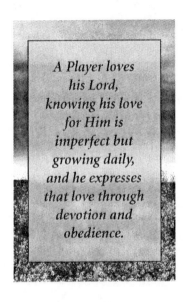

A Player loves his Lord, knowing his love for Him is imperfect but growing daily, and he expresses that love through devotion and obedience.

You began disciplining your brain as well, by recommitting yourself daily to purity, and by reviewing the reasons you're motivated to stay sober. In response to the chaos of your prior sin, you established order.

Allies became part of your process, as you realized rebuilding was never meant to be a solitary event. You formed alliances with brothers who share your vision, and you began reaping the benefit of their integrity combined with your own.

When necessary, you tried to restore the relationships injured by your sin. You expressed sorrow and acknowledged transgressions. Hoping to rebuild broken trust, you kneeled, humbly and simply, like the prodigal son owning his wrong.

As a steward of your body and all it contains, you've gotten a better understanding of the triggers in the environment that challenge you, the arena you strive in, the opponent you battle, the wounds you nurse, and the cycles of temptation you resist. Armed with fresh insight, you're ready to train.

Aware of relentless opposition, you've developed techniques to use when resisting. You've also applied an athlete's mind-set to correcting either your own entitled thinking or the violation of boundaries that have been disrupting your relationships. You've confronted yourself and, if necessary, others as well.

You're committed to longevity, though a relapse plan is in place because not having one seems foolhardy. And you're drawing meaning from your experience as a Player, a conqueror, and a lover of God.

When a man experiences the divine interruption, he learns hard lessons, seeing parts of himself he never knew existed. But reclaiming created intent begins and ends with God, not man. So it's only fitting that the process ends with man seeing Him, not himself. Then he experiences a new beginning as a servant seeing his Lord more clearly than ever.

Peter did. Of all the disciples, I relate best to him. He's a simple guy, earnest and impulsive, who tries hard and fails big. Looking at his life and process, I see so much of mine—so much of *ours*, I think—that I want to spend today reviewing Peter's experience as a man who is called, then as a man in crisis, and finally, as a man confirmed in the grace of God. So much of his process is our own: high expectations, lack of self-awareness, failure, grief, and despair. Then finally, when all seems lost, Peter experiences epiphany: a new beginning. His story connects with us, because it's our story too.

THE SERVANT CALLED

When Christ called Peter, He took him away from what seemed an ordinary life and invited him to high adventure. Look at some of Peter's experiences after he responded to Jesus's invitation to follow Him: his mother-in-law is miraculously healed (Matthew 8:14–15), he receives divine revelation about the Messiah (Matthew 16:16–19), he witnesses Jesus talking with Moses and Elijah (Luke 9:28–33), and he walks on water (Matthew 14:28–31).

Of course, Peter loved Jesus—what man wouldn't love a Master who took him for a ride like that? Not that the miraculous was all he cared for, of course. Like us, he loved Christ for many reasons, and he was a devoted yet imperfect follower.

You've had your own experiences with Christ, haven't you? Times He called you, when you knew He was inviting you into fellowship, discipleship, and adventure. No one can take these moments away from you. Like Peter, you have them burned into your heart. And because of that, you'd be wounded and angry if anyone suggested your love for Him wouldn't stand the test.

Peter was angry when someone suggested that to him. Problem was, it was Jesus Himself who said it. That had to have hurt deeply. When Jesus predicted all His disciples—Peter included—would forsake Him under pressure, you can almost hear the injury in Peter's voice when he protests: "Even if all are made to stumble because of You, I will never be made to stumble . . . Even if I have to die with You, I will not deny You!" (Matthew 26:33, 35).

I think Peter meant it. Sure, it was an extravagant thing to say. Arrogant, too, because he separated himself from the others by boasting that, in essence, he was a more devoted follower than they were. But he also sounds like a man offended and hurt that his Master thought so little of him as to suggest he'd let Him down in such a cowardly way. "I love You!" he seems to protest. "I don't have it in me to do a thing like that!"

Poor Peter—he meant that too. What a crushing blow Satan would strike, using those very words as a club.

Jesus saw what was coming, and He gently warned Peter, "Satan has asked for you, that he may sift you as wheat. But I have prayed for you, that your faith should not fail; and when you have returned to Me, strengthen your brethren" (Luke 22:31–32).

Bear with me while I paraphrase three things Jesus tries to convey to Peter here:

"First, Satan heard that. He'll throw your promise back in your face after you fail to keep it, and you'll enter the darkest period of your life.

"Second, when it all comes down in a few hours, try to remember this—I'm still on your side. I've prayed for you. Soon even you won't be on your side, but I will. You say you love Me too much to deny Me? Peter, I love you too much to deny you, and I won't—not now, not ever.

"And finally, when it's all over, use it! When you've failed spectacularly and repented bitterly, don't bury this experience. Use it to strengthen others."

Did Peter get it? I don't think so. With the benefit of hindsight, you and I can laugh at these guys and their inability to see the big picture, but would we have done differently?

Probably not. Remember, these had been heady times for Jesus's followers. They'd seen the dead raised, the crowds drawn, the miracles performed, the Pharisees rebuked, and the elements tamed. And all by their Man.

They had, in other words, good reason to believe the Messiah was finally here, ready to overturn Roman rule and establish the kingdom. And given what we know of man's ambition in general and Peter's in particular, it couldn't have escaped his attention that he was on the ground floor of this new venture. He seemed to have the inside track for the VP position—hadn't Jesus Himself called Peter "blessed" in front of all the others?—and life was going to be very, very good.

The servant was called and committed, but he was miserably unprepared for the test.

THE SERVANT IN CRISIS

Have you ever, in the aftermath of a brutal failure, asked yourself repeatedly where you went wrong or what you could have done differently?

Maybe you had an external crisis of truth (which is my diplomatic way of saying you got busted) and had to 'fess up, ashamed and bewildered, wondering how you ever got yourself into such a mess. Or maybe you said or did something so stupid you wonder where you left your head when you did it.

Magnify how you felt at those times by several hundred, and you get a sense of what Peter went through that night. I can easily envision him hashing it out after the Crucifixion, when all the disciples had gone into hiding. Lonely, embittered, frightened, and unspeakably disappointed, he turns on himself for the thousandth time:

"Fool! Why didn't I see it coming? He warned me, and I thought this time He really had it wrong. He seemed so moody anyway, I couldn't make out half of what He was saying.

"Then He needed me. He asked me to pray with Him and God curse me, I just conked out. I was too sleepy; it was too much trouble.

"Oh, Jesus, what I wouldn't give to lose twenty nights' sleep to pray with You, just once! You needed me, I let You down, but I swear I didn't know what You were facing. Do one last miracle and turn back time, and I'll crawl over rocks to pray with You!

"Then they came, and I panicked. They took Him, and I didn't mean to follow so far behind. But it was dark, I was scared, and I'd never seen so much hatred. Still, I thought I could handle it when I sat down with them, and then they asked me if I knew Him, and . . .

"I can't say it. But I did it—I did something I never thought a follower of Jesus Christ could do. Then I did it again, then again. And now I know, and I can't stand to know it; I don't want to know it. But I know it anyway.

"I'm not the man I thought I was.

"God help me, God forgive me, I am not the man I thought I was."

So, alone and humiliated, Peter hides.

If this were fiction, I'd say this would be the place to end it. It's the story of a very sad man who hoped too hard, tried, and failed. The end.

But, of course, this is neither fiction nor the end.

THE SERVANT CONFIRMED

Resurrection day—Easter morning, the blinding light, the empty tomb. Awesome, amazing.

But a tiny element of the story often gets lost—well, tiny to most, but enormous to our Peter.

When Mary Magdalene, Salome, and Christ's mother went to the tomb to anoint His body, an angel was there, announcing Christ's resurrection. And he gave the astonished women instructions that say volumes about the heart of God: "But go, tell His disciples—*and Peter*—that He is going before you to Galilee" (Mark 16:7; emphasis added).

And Peter . . . and *Peter!*

Can you see it? The angel, under orders from God, singles out Peter: "Tell His disciples—and Peter." Why does he specifically mention Peter? Because God knows the frailty of His servant.

"Tell Peter, because when he hears Jesus wants to see His disciples, Peter will assume that doesn't include him. Remind him that it does! Go to Peter—self-hating, despairing, frightened, and humiliated Peter—and tell him the Lord is not only risen but is thinking of him."

The Lord considers His weak, erring servants, thinking of us long after we've stopped thinking of Him. Then came the reconciliation between Jesus and His disciples, the explanation of the big picture, the new vision.

And finally, at the end of John's Gospel, a brief dialogue between Peter and his Lord is both his final breaking and his *making*: "Simon, son of Jonah, do you love Me more than these?" (John 21:15).

We lose something here in our modern translation. When Jesus said, "Do you love Me?" He asked in Greek, "Do you *agape* Me?" (As in, "Do you love Me with divine, perfect love?")

Peter's in a terrible position. The answer should be, "Of course I *agape* You! I love You with nothing less than God's perfect love!"

That's what it should be, but it isn't. And Peter now knows better than to make promises to Jesus he can't keep. Sadly, I'll bet even timidly, he replies, "I *phileo* You." The Greek word *phileo* means brotherly affection, human affection. In other words, Peter says, "In response to Your question, no. I do not *agape* You. I should say I do, but I've shot my mouth off before and I won't do it again. I'm an imperfect man who loves You imperfectly, so I *phileo* You—I care, but hard experience has proven I don't care nearly as much as I should."

Jesus repeats the question again; again, Peter gives an honest, though far from ideal, response.

Then Jesus repeats the question but replaces one word: "Simon, do you *phileo* Me?"

You can almost hear His tone: "Simon, is this the best you offer

Me? *Phileo*? After all I've done for you, you offer Me this? *Phileo* instead of *agape*?"

My uncle Joe served with troops that liberated a number of Europe's concentration camps during World War II. At Birkenau, he recalled, as prisoners streamed out of the barbed-wire compound, many of them were downright worshipful of the soldiers, seeing them as saviors. A Polish man approached Joe in that manner, speaking a language he couldn't understand, trying to convey indescribable gratitude.

Joe shook his head and shrugged; they couldn't communicate.

The man finally went silent, then ripped a button off his threadbare shirt and pressed it into my uncle's hand.

My uncle didn't need that button. And he cherished that button. It was given out of complete wretchedness, the faltering gift of a man trying to express feelings beyond words. It was nothing, and it was priceless.

Peter, now grieved, according to John's Gospel, offered his button: "Lord, You know all things. I *phileo* You."

The faltering gift of a man trying to express feelings beyond words.

"It's all I have," he seems to say. "It's nothing; You don't need it. Refuse it and I'll understand. But if there's still anything in You that can see anything in me that You could want, then it would mean everything to me—*everything!*—if You'd accept this button."

I know why you relate. The same reason I do. What else have we ever offered Him, really, if not a measly button?

Jesus overwhelms His servant with a confirmation: "When you were younger, you girded yourself and walked where you wished; but when you are old, you will stretch out your hands, and another will gird you and carry you where you do not wish" (John 21:18).

He was speaking, we know, of the way Peter would die. But was He not also describing the way Peter would, from now on, live? No longer his own; no longer the self-willed fisherman who girds himself and goes where he pleases. He's tried, failed, been humiliated and broken, then forgiven and blessedly, amazingly restored.

And weeks later, on the Day of Pentecost, he'll preach the sermon launching the history of the early church.

You may have seen a side of yourself you didn't want to see when you had your crisis of truth. It may have been breaking—for all I know, you may still be facing hard, breaking circumstances— but through them, we see a side of Him we've never seen. Because in our failure He meets us, reconfirming His desire for our intimacy and service, accepting our limitations, and requiring us to do the same.

He's prayed for you. Satan wanted you, but you were spoken for. Both of them—your Savior and your opponent—watched while you failed. One accused you; the other sought you out and restored you.

So take to heart what He said to His other servant. When you are converted, strengthen your brethren. Stay the course and let another take the reins of your life from now on. And go take that button you offered Him, which He definitely received, and let it be the gift He breaks and multiplies like bread to feed the multitudes.

They're waiting, the world's your arena, and The Game Plan's in place.

So go, Player. In Jesus's name, go.

DAY 30

ACTION PLAN FOR EPIPHANY

KEY VERSE

So when they had eaten breakfast, Jesus said to Simon Peter, "Simon, son of Jonah, do you love Me more than these?"

—JOHN 21:15

PRINCIPLE

The first commandment is to love God. Everything else—personal responsibility, relational integrity, sexual sobriety—should spring from your love for God and desire to please Him. It's often true, though, that a Player needs to be broken so that he can experience God's grace and restoration at the deepest level. Only then does his love for Him become what it is meant to be.

ACTION

1. Reconsider Peter's process in light of all you've been through these past thirty days.

   a. He was called from one way of life to another.

   b. He was a believer who was sure he loved Jesus.

   c. He overestimated his strength and underestimated the pressures the world and Satan would put on him.

   d. He compromised, crossed the line, and failed.

   e. He despaired.

   f. He was restored only after he faced his limitations and Christ's unlimited purposes and love for him.

2. Now look at your life and review points a through f. Apply each point to a historic point in your own life. When, where, and how did each one happen to you?

3. You've been broken, forgiven, and commissioned. What effect has this had on your thoughts of Christ and your heart toward Him?

RATIONALE

These thirty days are over, but you're just starting. By now, you should be equipped not just for purity but for service, intimacy, and a deeper bond with Christ. Ultimately, the deepening of that bond is the most important part of this process we call The Game. So if playing it helps you maintain your sexual integrity, amen to that. If it enhances strong accountability bonds between you and the men in your local Christian community, that's great. And if it helps restore trust and peace in your home, thank God.

But more than anything, The Game Plan was designed to re-establish you with Him, because nothing can matter more than your fulfilling the first and greatest commandment: "Love the LORD your God with all your heart, with all your soul, and with all your mind" (Matthew 22:37).

May your life always be lived in love with Him.

PRAYER

I am Your son, Your creation, Your redeemed servant to whom You've shown endless mercy and favor. I've been corrected when I've compromised, reestablished when I've wandered, reconciled with You when I've rebelled. And all because your thoughts toward me are thoughts of peace, not evil, to bring me to an expected end.

So what more can I say? Only this: whatever the "expected end" is You have in mind for me, let nothing—not the world, the devil, or myself—ever hinder Your purposes, and may that end be fulfilled in me, in spite of me, by You. I ask this in Jesus's name. Amen.

APPENDIX

QUESTIONS PLAYERS FREQUENTLY ASK

ACCOUNTABILITY

"CAN MY WIFE BE MY ACCOUNTABILITY PARTNER?"

Not a good idea. She has her hands full just being your wife, so let's not add accountability to her list of responsibilities. Making her your partner will almost certainly create a mother/son dynamic in your marriage, which cannot be healthy. So let your wife be your life partner, and let another man commit to being your accountability partner.

"IF THERE'S NO ACCOUNTABILITY GROUP AVAILABLE IN MY AREA, SHOULD I START ONE MYSELF? IF SO, HOW DO I GO ABOUT STARTING IT?"

In general, it's best to join an existing group rather than start one yourself. But if there really is nothing available in your area, you might consider taking the following steps:

First, consult with your pastor, and get his blessing and permission to begin facilitating a group. Ask if he or any staff member would be willing to lead it; if not, then you may need to facilitate it yourself. With your pastor, determine where and when your meetings will take place and how to let your church know about the formation of your group.

Second, during your group meetings, use a book such as this one. That will give you a format and good educational material.

Finally, stay in close communication with someone who has experience in this area as you begin your group. You'll need guidance and encouragement, so be sure to stay connected.

ADDICTION

"I HEAR THE TERM *SEXUAL ADDICTION* QUITE A BIT. WHAT QUALIFIES A MAN AS A 'SEX ADDICT'? HOW WOULD I KNOW IF I AM ONE?"

Sexual addiction is a relatively new term, generally used to describe a pattern of sexual acting out that's gotten way out of control.

Comparing the term to *alcoholism* can make it easier to understand. Drunkenness is a serious sin, but plenty of guys get drunk occasionally who are not alcoholics—that is, they haven't developed a dependency on the alcohol. The same is true of sexual addiction—not every man who sexually sins is a sex addict. Neither does a strong sex drive indicate sexual addiction.

Generally, if a man's sexual sin has increased in frequency and intensity; has intruded into his finances, family life, and professional life; and has become a life-dominating behavior that he's tried many times to stop and hasn't, then it fits the description of addictive behavior.

"BUT ISN'T IT WRONG TO IDENTIFY YOURSELF AS A 'SEX ADDICT' IF YOU'RE A CHRISTIAN?"

If you adopt any recovery term as your primary identification, then of course, that's wrong. As a Christian, your primary identification is in Christ. You're also a man, a human, and a citizen, all of which helps define you.

But if you are addicted to a certain behavior and recognize it, that does not in any way negate or discount your primary identification in Christ. It's simply a way of recognizing an aspect of your life that needs ongoing attention.

By way of example, remember that the apostle Paul identified himself several different ways: apostle, teacher, sinner, Jew, servant of God. He also identified himself as a man with a problem that he prayed about but was never fully delivered from, a problem he referred to as a "thorn in the flesh." (Read 2 Corinthians 12.) Whatever Paul's "thorn" was, he *recognized* it without making it his *primary identification*. That's the difference.

You are, first and foremost, a child of God. If you also happen to be sexually addicted, it's wise to recognize that as well, so you take appropriate action to keep the addiction from running your life.

"WHAT DO YOU THINK OF TWELVE-STEP PROGRAMS LIKE ALCOHOLICS ANONYMOUS OR SEXAHOLICS ANONYMOUS?"

Although this book is not written from a Twelve-Step perspective, I believe Twelve-Step programs can provide practical, useful ways to manage your sexual desires and behavior—provided you recognize that it is a secular program that respects, but does not promote, a specifically Christian, Bible-based approach.

I also recognize that the Twelve-Step approach isn't for everyone, and I don't consider it to be the only viable approach to addiction or life-dominating behavior. It's one of many valuable resources a man can avail himself of. But be certain that, above all else, you're reading the Bible daily; making prayer a daily habit; attending a Bible-believing, Christ-centered church; and establishing close ties with other believers. That's your foundation—never allow any secular or group support program to replace it.

MARRIAGE

"IF I'VE ACTED OUT SEXUALLY, SHOULD I TELL MY WIFE?"

If a husband has used pornography or has had adulterous relations, I believe he *should* tell his wife for the following reasons:

First, she is entitled to know. He's broken his marital covenant with his wife, and that's information she has a right to know and deal with, no matter how painful the knowledge may be.

Second, experience has shown that, in more cases than not, the wife already knows that something is wrong. Often, she senses that adultery is the problem, even if she has no concrete evidence of it. So when a husband doesn't come clean, she's left with a strong feeling that something's wrong; and, compounding the problem, she senses that her husband isn't willing to be honest about whatever it is that's wrong. She's in the dark, knowing that there's a problem but also knowing that her man isn't willing to deal with it. And that's a terrible position for any wife to be in.

Finally, experience shows that when a man keeps such an important secret from his wife, it affects their general intimacy. He's covering up, withholding important information, hoping she won't catch him. That can't help but poison the marriage. It also makes it easier for the man to continue in secret sexual sin, because by keeping the sin hidden, the man avoids the sort of consequence and accountability he needs to abandon that behavior. All in all, then, I'm convinced a man should disclose his sexual sin to his wife and, together with his wife, seek to rebuild the marital intimacy his sin has weakened.

"SOME TEACHERS SAY THAT IF A MARRIED MAN HAS BEEN INVOLVED IN SEXUAL SIN, THEN HE AND HIS WIFE NEED TO ABSTAIN FROM SEX FOR NINETY DAYS. DO YOU AGREE?"

In some cases, abstaining from marital relations is a very good approach. If a man has saturated himself with pornography, for example, he may have difficulty responding to his wife sexually without relying on pornographic fantasies. In that case, he may need to "dry out" so he can respond to normal stimulation without relying on the intensity of pornography.

But other cases may not require abstinence; and in some cases, it may actually damage the bond that a husband and wife need to rebuild. So the best approach is to take each case individually. If you're unsure whether you and your wife should abstain sexually, consult with a marriage counselor who can help you understand which approach is best suited to your situation.

"IS ORAL SEX BETWEEN HUSBAND AND WIFE A SIN? ARE THERE ANY SEXUAL ACTIVITIES THAT ARE 'OFF LIMITS' WITHIN MARRIAGE?"

There are no Bible verses declaring certain sexual acts "off limits" between husband and wife. But there are biblical principles that make some sexual practices inherently wrong or inappropriate, even within marriage.

Pornography, for example, is always wrong. Some couples try to incorporate the viewing of adult videos into their sex life to "spice it up," but this violates the biblical principle of monogamy, or sexual fidelity. Since Jesus condemned lust as a form of internal adultery (Matthew 5:27–28), the use of pornography is never allowable and is absolutely off limits.

Likewise, any practice that requires fantasy, such as sadomasochism or role-playing, violates the principle of intimate unity within marriage, because such practices encourage each partner to be someone other than who he or she really is. So any behavior that doesn't enhance genuine closeness between husband and wife is, according to this principle, inappropriate.

Any practice that harms the body through cutting, bruising, or unhygienic activity (bondage, sadomasochism, or anal intercourse) violates the principle of properly stewarding God's temple (1 Corinthians 6:19) and is therefore, in my opinion, also wrong.

Regarding oral sex, nothing in Scripture forbids it or even specifically mentions it. Oral sex can be, therefore, a legitimate form of marital pleasure, provided both parties are comfortable with it and enjoy it. But if a husband is coercing his wife into this practice (or vice versa) even though she's uncomfortable doing it, then he is violating the principle of mutual respect and benevolence (1 Corinthians 7:3–5; Ephesians 5:22–25), making the practice of oral sex, in this case, off limits.

Within these guidelines, married couples have tremendous liberty to express themselves freely. Take some time to read the entire Song of Solomon—a graphically beautiful depiction of marital love—and keep in mind the nobility that Scripture bestows on sex within marriage: "Marriage is honorable among all, and the bed undefiled" (Hebrews 13:4).

"MY WIFE SAYS THAT MY USE OF PORNOGRAPHY CONSTITUTES ADULTERY. DOES IT? IF SO, DOES SHE HAVE THE OPTION TO FILE FOR DIVORCE?"

Since the divorce question is one of the most contentious issues modern Christians face, you'll hear several different responses to this question. Let me give you mine.

My opinion is that pornography does *not* constitute adultery and, for that reason, does not constitute biblical grounds for divorce. Remember that when Jesus compared lust to adultery in Matthew 5:28, He stated, "I say to you that whoever looks at a woman to lust for her has already committed adultery with her *in his heart*" (emphasis added).

He later stated, in Matthew 19:9: "Whoever divorces his wife, except for sexual immorality, and marries another, commits adultery; and whoever marries her who is divorced commits adultery."

By combining these two scriptures, some have assumed Jesus meant that a spouse's adultery was just grounds for divorce and that lust, even without action, constituted literal adultery, so lust alone was grounds for a husband or wife to file for divorce.

Yet Jesus did make the distinction between adultery of the heart and literal, physical adultery. Both are sins, to be sure, and both should be taken seriously. But the consequences of the two are different, as should a spouse's response be.

Compare this to what John stated in his epistle regarding murder. In 1 John 3:15, he states, "Whoever hates his brother is a murderer." Here John clearly says there are two different types of murder: literal and internal. Both are serious, but our response to each is different. No reasonable person would suggest the death penalty be applied to someone who hates, even though hatred is a form of murder. The two are clearly different. I, for one, would much rather be murdered in someone's heart than literally killed!

So it is with adultery. Adultery of the heart is a grievous sin, but to count it the same as physical adultery—a literal sexual encounter with another person as opposed to lust or sexual fantasy—is, to my thinking, as absurd as counting hatred the same as the literal killing of another human being.

Having said this, let me add that, at times, I have advised a wife to separate from her husband because of his ongoing use of pornography. Children are endangered by this product, as they may well find their father's porn or walk in on him as he's viewing it. And the man who uses it insults his wife and defiles his home. So if he refuses to abandon it, the wife may have no choice but to have him removed from the home unless and until he gives up the habit. But again, this constitutes temporary separation, not divorce.

MASTURBATION

"I WANT TO STOP MASTURBATING, BUT IT SEEMS IMPOSSIBLE. HOW CAN I DO IT?"

The bad news is, there's no tried-and-true technique. A combination of prayer, impulse control, and strategy is the only approach I know of that works.

First, be patient and realistic. Most men who try to stop masturbating don't stop immediately. View this the way you would view a sin like pride or laziness. These are sins you may occasionally commit, then confess, then try the next time around not to yield to. So keep masturbation in perspective. Then put all of the following practices in place:

- Obviously, pray for strength.

- Let your accountability partner and group know of your commitment and ask them to hold you accountable.

- Determine when you're most tempted to masturbate. (For most guys it's either right before sleeping or when they wake up with an erection.) Be sure to pray at those times, and do some extra Bible reading to cleanse your mind.

- Be especially careful about your television habits. Everything you take in visually will help or hinder you.

- Be aware that your body will "lie" to you, telling you that you have to have an orgasm. You don't. You're just used to it on a regular basis, so you're craving it.

- When the urge hits, think long and hard about the impulse control you're trying to develop and the long-range benefits it yields. Remember and recite the verse on page 142 that you use for the distraction technique.

- Try always to be in the middle of a good book that can help distract your thoughts.

- Let your body release itself naturally. If you have a "wet dream," there's nothing wrong with that—it's a natural form of release that you'll probably have regularly.

- If you're married, make sure you and your wife are keeping your sex life regular. Make it more frequent, in fact, if possible.

PSYCHOLOGY

"SHOULD I SEE A PSYCHOLOGIST OR PROFESSIONAL COUNSELOR FOR MY SEXUAL PROBLEM?"

A man who has sexually sinned doesn't automatically need professional help. But if you are in extreme emotional pain, are having a difficult time either rebuilding or keeping relationships, or your marriage is in serious trouble, then a professional counselor could be very helpful.

Make sure, though, he counsels from a biblical perspective. And calling himself a Christian counselor does not guarantee that he uses a biblical perspective, so ask him these specific questions before you sign up for ongoing counseling:

1. Are you an active member of a local church?

2. What role does the Bible play in the counsel you give?

3. What is your approach when dealing with a Christian man who has gotten involved in sexual sin?

A good rule of thumb to adopt, by the way, when judging any psychological theory is this: If it is confirmed in Scripture, embrace it. If it is contradicted by Scripture, reject it. If it is neither confirmed nor contradicted in Scripture, consider it the way you would any unprovable theory—possibly true worth at least considering.

"IF I HAVE DEEP EMOTIONAL CONFLICTS THAT ARE CONTRIBUTING TO MY SEXUAL SIN, HOW CAN I IDENTIFY THEM?"

The sort of conflicts that often contribute to sexual sin—deeply ingrained rage, for example, or isolation or fear of intimacy—are best identified through a combination of self-examination and communication.

First, self-examination. Look at the mood or emotional state that you were in the last several times you sexually sinned or acted out. You may see a pattern that can help you identify conflicts that make you vulnerable. Lots of men act out when they're lonely, which indicates a problem with normal intimacy. Others tend to act out when they're angry, which might indicate a problem dealing directly with anger and confrontation. So look for patterns in your history, and try to learn from them.

Then communicate with a pastor or Christian counselor who can work with you on identifying whatever problems you may have relating to others or to yourself. Communicate with your friends and loved ones by asking them to give you honest feedback about yourself and the way you relate to them. And of course, communicate with God. Join with David in his prayer that God would bring to light whatever secret, hidden sins you have that need attention (Psalm 19:12–13). That's a prayer I trust God will be all too happy to answer.

SALVATION

"HOW DO I REALLY KNOW I'M SAVED? I'VE NEVER BEEN SURE."

Let me go over some basic points with you about sin and salvation, along with some relevant scriptures.

- Sin, which is universal, falls short of what our Creator intended for us. "All have sinned and fall short of the glory of God" (Romans 3:23).

- As a result all of us, whether hetero- or homosexual, are under a death sentence. "The wages of sin is death [eternal separation from God]" (Romans 6:23).

- Yet God wants us in His family. "But God demonstrates His love toward us, in that while we were still sinners, Christ died for us" (Romans 5:8).

- Our part is to say yes to this unchanging invitation. "If you confess with your mouth the Lord Jesus and believe in your heart that God has raised Him from the dead, you will be saved" (Romans 10:9).

If you have any doubt as to whether or not you belong to Christ and are ready to meet Him, pray this prayer:

Lord Jesus, when I look at this imperfect world, it reminds me that I, too, am imperfect. I understand that it was for my sins that You suffered. Thank You for Your sacrifice and for loving me no matter what I've done or where I've been. Please forgive me of my sins. I want to turn my life around and begin life anew with You as my Lord and Savior. Thank You for conquering sin and death so that I can have eternal life with You. I ask this in Jesus's name. Amen.

If you prayed this prayer, be certain to find a local, Bible-believing church to attend this week. Meet with the pastor or a staff member, and let him know that you just received Christ and that you want to know what steps you should now take.

Welcome to the family of God!

NOTES

1. R. Jamieson, A. R. Fausset, and David Brown's, *Commentary on the Whole Bible* (Grand Rapids: Zondervan, 1961), 1206.

2. A nationwide survey of 1,031 adults conducted by Zogby International and Focus on the Family, dated March 8–10, 2000, reported in "Zogby/Focus Survey Reveals Shocking Internet Sex Statistics," *Legal Facts: Family Research Council*, vol. 2. no. 20 (30 March 2000).

3. Kenneth Woodward, "Sex, Morality and the Protestant Minister," *Newsweek*, 28 July 1997, 62.

4. "Pornography Addiction: A Stronghold Inside Church Walls Too," www.CrossWalk.com (20 July 2001).

5. Tim Wilkins, "First Person: How to Surf the Internet and Avoid Wiping Out to Porn," Baptist Press News, October 30, 2003.

6. Charles R. Swindoll, *David: A Man of Passion and Destiny* (Nashville: W Publishing Group, 1997), 77.

7. James Dobson, *Focus on the Family* video series (Waco, TX: Word Publishing, 1978).

8. Dr. Dwight Carlson, *From Guilt to Grace* (Eugene, Ore.: Harvest House, 1986), 91.

9. Dr. Erwin Lutzer, *Living with Your Passions* (Colorado Springs: Victor, 1983), 69–72.

10. Jack Hayford, "Solo Sex," *New Man* magazine, September/October 2003.

11. John Maxwell, *The Maxwell Leadership Bible* (Nashville: Nelson Bibles, 2003), 582.

12. Martin Luther King, Jr. on "Forgiveness." Quoted in *Graham's Homepage*, www.weeks-g.dircon.couk/index.html.

13. C. S. Lewis, "Dying to Self," *The Weight of Glory* (San Francisco: HarperSanFrancisco, 2001 reprint), 190.

14. Francis Schaeffer, *True Spirituality* (Carol Stream, Ill.: Tyndale, 1979), 26–27.

15. Rick Warren, *The Purpose Driven Life* (Grand Rapids: Zondervan, 2002).

16. Viktor Frankl, *Man's Search for Meaning* (Boston: Beacon Press, revised 1997).

17. Warren, *The Purpose Driven Life*, 291.

18. Jim Bakker, *I Was Wrong* (Nashville: Thomas Nelson, 1996).

19. Bishop William Fry, quoted in "Church and Society," *Time*, 24 June 1991, 49.

To contact Joe Dallas for speaking engagements or products, please contact:

JOE DALLAS

GENESIS COUNSELING

17632 IRVINE BLVD. SUITE #220
TUSTIN, CA 92780

714-508-6953

WWW.GENESISCOUNSELING.ORG